From A Boy to a Godly Man

A Boy's Bible Study of David

by

Katy
Foster

S0-BZM-776

Additional Insights by
Christopher Foster

From A Boy to a Godly Man
A Boy's Bible Study of David
By Katy Foster
Coauthored by Christopher Foster

All rights reserved. No part of this book may be reproduced or transmitted in any form or by any means, electronic or mechanical, including photocopying, recording or by any information storage and retrieval system, without written permission from the author, except for the inclusion of brief quotations in a review.

Copyright © 2014 by Katy Foster and Christopher Foster
2nd edition
All rights reserved.
ISBN 13 – 9781495970450
ISBN 10 - 1495970450

Scripture taken from the New King James Version®. Copyright © 1982 by Thomas Nelson. Used by permission.

Permissions granted for use of the following photos:

"rocky path"© Georgi Radev/Stockvault Photos; "clock"© Andres Rodriguez/Dreamstime Photos; "sheep" © Rud/Dreamstime Stock Photos; "cross" © David R. Grainger/Stockvault Photos; "world map" © Nicholas Raymond/ Stockvault Photos; "church" © DFNatureAwed/Stockvault Photos; "cross" © DreamWarrior/Stockvault Photos; "silhouette of people" © 2happy/ Stockvault Photos; "scripture" © Heather E. Kitchen/Stockvault Photos; "dove" © Boris Kyurkchiev/ Stockvault Photos; "crown" © johninportland/Morguefile; "hands shaking"© Chris Moncrieff/Dreamstime Photos; "boys on shore" © voldevis/Stockvault Photos.
All other photo and images were created by the author, Katy Foster, with all rights reserved as stated above.

Printed in the United States of America

In humility, my mind is flooded with precious names, beautiful faces, and sweet family members and friends that God has placed in my life:

Chris, Alex, Annabelle, Ansley, Mom, Dad, Linda, Kelly, Ric, Noah, Sam, Johnny, Hope, Landon,"Little Johnny," Melissa, Erick, & Josten, … and Hunter.

… all a big part of God's amazing grace!

I thank Jesus for being my biggest encouragement, and for always being my best friend.

For of Him and through Him and to Him are all things, to whom be glory forever. Amen.

Romans 11:36

TABLE OF CONTENTS

Chapter 1

Your Intro

You may already know a great deal about David. He is taught in every Sunday school class. Particularly the part about killing Goliath with a small stone. You've heard that, right? However, did you actually read that in the Bible yourself, or did you listen to your Sunday school teacher talk about it? It is not the same thing, nowhere near.

There's something unique and special about laying your eyes on the words from God's heart, that is, the Bible. As God inspired the words of the Bible to be written, He was thinking of what He knows *you* need to read and what *you* need to know. The words in the Bible are there so that you will come closer to Him, and in turn, become a man of God.

This book will guide you to read through the book of First Samuel and the first four chapters of Second Samuel. Be prepared to be changed by the Lord, not by this book, but by His Book.

This book will guide you to do what the Bible says. We are to be doers, not just hearers, as instructed in James 1:22. You will be doing God's Word in this study, not just reading it.

There are four important landmarks you will see as you travel through this book that have important meanings:

1. Throughout this study you will see the words "Live It!" which instructs you to *do* God's word, including scripture memorization. Let's try it now....

LIVE IT!

You will need a pack of index cards to write down memory verses that are all throughout this Bible study. Punch a hole in one corner of each index card and tie the cards together with a string or key ring. These are helpful as you try to memorize your verses. You can take these cards with you on road trips and see how many verses you can memorize. You can take these cards anywhere, such as school, grandparent's house, friend's house, doctor's office, to church, or anywhere.

Do index cards seem a bit old-fashioned and out-of-date to you? If so, using an electronic device that you have access to can be just as effective to keep memory verses. There are a number of apps available where you can plug in your memory verses and then have easy access to them. Index cards or an electronic device . . . your choice. Have one and/or the other set and ready within the next couple of days.

2. A second important thing you will see in this study is a row of dots, like these:

· · · · · ·

These dots give you a stopping point for the day. Some lessons are lengthy, or need more time to reflect and spend with God; therefore, it is not necessary to complete an entire lesson in one day. Stop for the day when you get to these dots. The next day, be sure to review what you studied each previous day as a reminder and warm-up.

3. The third important part of this book that you will see is called *"The Way I See It..."* These are commentaries written by a wonderful, genuine, and honest man of God, Christopher Foster. He gives his own "manly" perspectives of the Bible verses you will be studying.

4. Last important landmark: there is a map at the beginning of every following chapter. Each map is of Israel, but shows only the cities and territories that you will read about in each chapter of the Bible. Use the maps to give you a better understanding of where everything is going on.

Lesson 1

Building the Foundations

God knows about the difficulties of being a growing boy. He knows all about it completely. He knows just how bad every pain hurts, every cut, every bruise, every sickness, and every broken bone. Then there are those other pains, like loneliness, hurt feelings, fear, frustration, embarrassment, anger, and sadness. God knows just how bad those pains hurt, too.

God also knows all about what makes your heart leap for joy. He knows what you love. He knows who you love. He knows all about it. Actually, God knows more about what makes you smile, what makes you laugh, dance, jump, and what gives you that sparkle in your eye and that full joy in your heart more than *you* know!

What do you believe? Do you believe God knows more about your joys and your pains, more than you? If you answer yes, that is what's called *"blessed assurance!"* Not only did you answer correctly, but you also have a very important and crucial knowledge of God… ***He knows!***

Furthermore, God wants to show you how *He* sees you and what He sees through His eyes. That's pretty cool – to have the opportunity to see something the way God sees it cannot compare to anything! Think about it, being so close to God that you actually see people and events in the world and things around you in the same way the Highest of High, the Creator, the Kings of Kings sees things. When God does give us a glimpse through His eyes, we will be closer to Him, and God knows that being close to Him **is the greatest joy you can possibly have!**

It is important for you to know not only that God knows, but also that He loves you so much, He wants you to know, too!

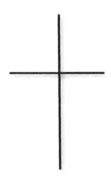

This does not mean God wants you to know what a broken arm feels like. God wants you to know how to avoid and deal with pains. When you do have pains (and you will), God wants you to know how to deal with this pain and how to grow from the pain. He wants you to know so fully the joy you can have in your life that in times of pain, you know that *joy is still there!*

This is not impossible, feeling joy in pain, that is. God wants you to know it. He wants you to know because it is a beautiful thing to know. First, you've got to know about His love. . .

God is holy, which means perfect and without sin. We are, well, not perfect. Far from it, actually. It stems back from the first sinners, Adam and Eve, and it has made its way into your heart and everyone else's hearts. God killed an animal, took its skin, and covered Adam and Eve with the skin. The sin was covered and paid for by the sacrificed animal, and a relationship with God continued. The animal was a sacrifice for the sin. The animal did not do anything wrong, yet it lost its life for the sins of others. Then, God promised that One would come as a sacrifice for all the sins of all people. Jesus, God's own Son, was this sacrifice. God did this because He wants to have a relationship with you. He wants you to believe in Jesus so you can know how to live, and how to live forever. The only way to having a relationship with God is believing that Jesus lovingly and fully paid for your sins as a sacrifice, and choosing to follow Him. Jesus is the only way, and God really wants you to know. If you do believe, here is how God sees you: His perfect child, washed clean from sin by the sacrifice of Jesus. As His child, He wants you to grow to be more like Him, your Father.

Lesson 2

You

How do you see yourself? With your eyes, in a mirror, right? OK, sure. But what do you see with those eyes? How would you describe your outward appearance? Write down 3 to 5 descriptions of you, your outward appearance:

_____

_____

_____

_____

_____

Now ask two other people you know to tell you 3 to 5 descriptions of your outward appearance. Perhaps just asking, "How do you think I look?" or "How would you describe me?" The two people can be absolutely anybody – parents, siblings, grandparents, neighbors, friends, or whomever. Write down their answers.

Person 1:

_____

_____

_____

_____

Person 2:

_____

_____

_____

_____

Did their descriptions of you match your own descriptions of you? Possibly similar, but more than likely, you got responses from others that you did not write down for yourself. You may even see opposite descriptions of you. You may have gotten descriptions that you disagree with, or descriptions that you do not like. Now that you have this information, it can give you an idea of how others perceive your outward appearance. You are able to see yourself through someone else's eyes.

Now try another activity. Write down 3 to 5 descriptions of your inward appearance. You can include how you describe your personality, your attitude, your character, your strengths, or maybe even your weaknesses.

_____

_____

_____

_____

_____

Once again, without telling your own answers, ask two people to give 3 to 5 descriptions of your inward appearance. Now remember, you cannot tell them what to say and what not to say. You cannot say, "You think I'm wonderful, don't you? Amazing? Maybe even perfect?" Also, no disapproving facial expressions if you do not like what they say. You cannot grit your teeth if your sister says you are mean. Just write it down without giving any comments. Write down their answers:

Person 1:   Person 2:

_____   _____

_____   _____

_____   _____

_____   _____

_____   _____

Once again, compare what you wrote to what others say. You may like what others say, and you may not. Whether or not you like it, this is how others see who you are. You have been given a chance to see through the eyes of others. You saw what they see.

As already mentioned, you may or may not like what others say. Furthermore, you may think they are wrong. They may be wrong. After all, they are not God, right? (Pause. You probably do not need to let little brother or sister know they are not God. This may just bring a little devilishness out.) God knows, and God's descriptive words of you are completely accurate.

Since God's description of you is completely accurate, wouldn't it be a treat to see yourself through God's eyes? If you can know how God sees you, then you will know what parts of your life need to strengthen and grow.

Or, better yet, wouldn't it be a treat to see *everything* through God's eyes, to see what gives Him joy, and to see what makes His heart break? Would you like to see through God's eyes? Hopefully, you answered yes, because you can!

Lesson 3

Four Steps

God will show you how He sees you. They are called the "Know-to-Grow Steps." These four steps are important for you to do absolutely every single day of your life. Here are the four steps:

1. Read your Bible,
2. Apply,
3. Obey, and
4. Pray.

These steps do not necessarily have to be done in this order. We will go through these four steps again and again in this Bible study. It will give you good practice in making this not a daily habit, but a *lifestyle*.

There is a difference between a habit and a lifestyle. A habit can be broken. Also, a habit does not make you who you are. You may have a habit of biting your nails, but that does not make you half-beaver.

A lifestyle may start off similar to a habit. It is something you choose to do often. However, the lifestyle grows into something more, something bigger, and it becomes part of you.

For example, learning to play an instrument requires daily practice. Then it can grow into a deeper love for music and a desire to make music with your instrument. Then you may become a musician. It becomes part of you. Or, you may love to run every day. Then, you start to appreciate growing strong legs and a strong heart and the refreshing feeling of running. Then you may be in races or a marathon. It becomes part of you.

Read

Apply

Obey

Pray

Walking through the Know-to-Grow steps every day will also become a lifestyle that will guide you closer to God and closer to knowing God. The more you know God, the more you will fall in love with Him, and the more you will want to be like Him, and He will show you how. It will become part of you. You will begin to see more of God every day. You will be amazed at how great He is. You will love having Him in your life, and you will want more of Him. You, like King David (finally, *there's* his name), will be a man after God's own heart!

Here is a deeper look at the four steps:

1. **Pray.** For this study, you will be instructed to pray at the end of the Bible Study. This, of course, does not mean you cannot pray before the Bible Study begins as well. It is good to ask for God's guidance before reading the Bible. The power of prayer will be the greatest thing you see in the entire Bible Study. At the close of each Bible time, you will be instructed to ask God to help you see through His eyes.

2. **Read your Bible.** Have your Bible ready to do this *Bible* study. Get ready to read what God has to say to you – yes, you!

3. **Apply.** As you read the Bible, think, "What does God want me to know about these verses?" Also, think about how the verses you read can help you right now, today. Applying the Bible is like applying sunscreen. God's Word will protect you from the harmful rays of sin. Then you can enjoy life and enjoy learning with the Son!

4. **Obey.** Once you have read God's word, you have been given guidance. This is where you have to be a doer. You may have to get up from your comfortable chair. This is no parade for you to watch. You are *in* the parade. You will not be nice and cozy in a blanket during this study. Always be ready to get up.

The Way I See It....

by Christopher Foster

The power of prayer and the power of God's Word are undeniable in our lives. For me, it is obvious when I am and am not in the Word and not having regular conversations with God. As I go through life and each day, I am faced with challenges that I can choose to either go at alone or lean on God for support. As a young man, and even now, I have a tendency to want to solve challenges on my own, because it seems easier. This is why it is important to develop a consistent relationship with God by praying regularly and reading His Word. By doing this, I begin a closer walk with God, making those everyday challenges easier to overcome. God has BIG plans for you and me, and the only way to understand and fulfill those plans is for us to stay strong in our walk with God through prayer and the reading of His Word.

Young man of God, you are now ready and equipped
to dive into I Samuel 1!

Samuel Bound!

Chapter 2

The Path along the Way

Anywhere you go, there is a path to be taken. You find yourself gazing out the window on the way to the grocery store, mesmerized by the trees, grass, the sky, and even the gas station. The path we take to get somewhere is filled with things to see.

Similarly, you are taking a path into manhood with every ticking second, like it or not. You cannot stop it, which is okay, because sweet brother in Christ, there are so many wonderful things to see!

Take our Lord and Savior Jesus Christ, for example. Jesus came, as the prophets proclaimed to be a sacrificial lamb. He came to die for us. However, the *path* of His life on earth along the way was amazing! His teachings cannot be compared to any other teacher that has ever lived. He was humble and poor, yet bold and courageous. Now here's the catcher: the life Jesus lived *paved* the path for God's will to be done. Jesus did not sit around for 30 years and then decide to do God's will. Jesus' every step, starting at birth, was a building block for God's will.

Today is a building block for you as well. Every day is a building block for you to live in God's will. Talk about pressure, right? Well, welcome to the beauty and worth of life. You are taking the path to God's will for you as a man of God, every single day, and you can make it an amazing, joyous journey along the way.

The lessons in Chapter 2 give information that build up to the anointing of King David. Enjoy and love your journey!

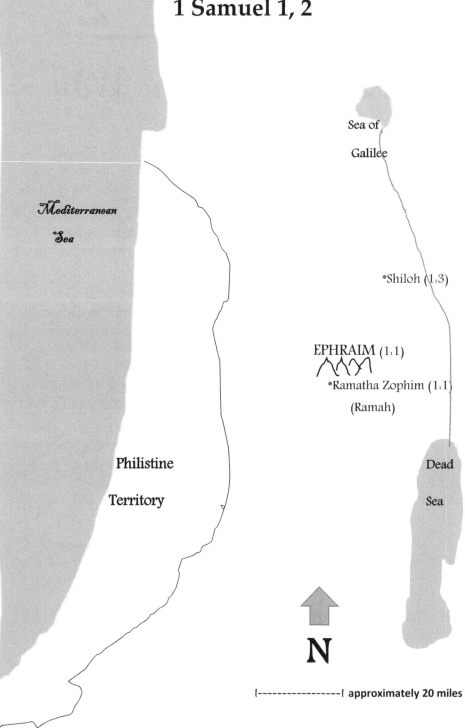

Israel

1 Samuel 1, 2

Sea of
Galilee

Mediterranean
Sea

*Shiloh (1:3)

EPHRAIM (1:1)

*Ramatha Zophim (1:1)

(Ramah)

Philistine

Territory

Dead

Sea

N

|--------------| approximately 20 miles

Lesson 1

Set the Stage

Day 1

Before we really dive into the life of David, we need to "set the stage."

READ I Samuel 1.

CHECK OUT THE MAP!

Explanations in your reading:

> v. 1   "Ramathaim Sophim" – This is the town where Elkanah and Hannah lived. From here on out, you will see this town referred to as "Ramah."

Write a summary and your own thoughts of the reading:

-Hannah prayed for a son and the Lord blessed her and then she named him Samuel

- Samuel grew to serve God and grew with God

• • • • • •

(Remember, you can stop for the day at the dots.)

Day 2

Many people are mentioned in the first chapter: Elkanah – a man from the Ehpraimite tribe. Ephraim was a son of Joseph and grandson of Israel (Jacob) in the book of Genesis. Of course, Ephraim is not in 1 Samuel and is long dead.

Elkanah's wife Hannah, desperately wanted to have a baby. God blessed her, and Hannah gave birth to a son. She named the baby boy Samuel. Samuel grew up in the temple, "the House of the LORD," with Eli, the priest. Samuel served God and grew with God.

Read

Apply

Obey

Pray

Apply & Obey

Hannah's prayer was heard by God, and He blessed her. Did Hannah then forget God, forget how desperately she prayed, and go her own way? No. She remembered God, and gave this great gift of a son back to God.

God has given you a Son as well, His only Son. What can you give back to God today?

LIVE IT!

Write it down. Ask parents/grandparents for help, only if needed.

Today for God, I give Him

my heart
_____

my goals
_____

_____

_____

LIVE IT!

Write out **Psalm 113:3** and memorize:

_____

_____

_____

_____

_____

Share the verse with three people and add the verse to your index cards and/or memory verse list.

_____

Pray by praising God and thanking Him for whatever may come to your mind. Ask Him to help you stay mindful of His many gifts He has given you. Ask God to help you see through His eyes.

_____

Lesson 2

Like an Island

Read I Samuel 2:1-26.

Write a summary of the reading and your own thoughts:

- Hanah's prayer
- Eli's sons
- Samuel's obediance
- Eli not restraining

_____

• • • • • •

Chapter 2 tells us Eli the priest had two sons that did not grow with God. As a matter of fact, they lived only for themselves, and the two brothers did whatever they wanted to do. They were wicked. They were evil. They chose not to grow with God. The Bible then again tells us that "Samuel grew before the LORD" (verse 26).

Samuel's decision to follow God was important, because God had a great plan for Samuel. God has a great plan for you, too!

Apply

Samuel was basically raised by Eli. So most likely Samuel and Eli's sons knew each other very well. How hard do you think it is to be surrounded by others that do not follow Jesus?

Write your thoughts:

It is difficult when you are talking about church but otherwise it isn't bad.

Can you still follow Jesus? That may be a hard question. You may be outnumbered by others who will not stand for Jesus, by praising a movie or TV show that defies the laws of God, by using rude words or bad language, or by acting unloving and uncaring toward others. They may expect you to participate, to have fun with them, to hang out. If you do not, you may be laughed at, sneered at, called names, or treated unfairly. The easiest thing to do is to sneer back, hit, and make them mad. In these moments, it is *essential* (which means a must) to have a Bible verse of comfort. Samuel surely had Joshua 1:9 hidden in his heart as he was growing with God.

LIVE IT!

Write **Joshua 1:9** and memorize:

• • • • • •

Day 3

Like Samuel, also hide this next verse in your heart. Write **Psalm 91:11, 12,** and memorize:

_____

_____

_____

_____

_____

_____

Once you have these two verses memorized, share them with three people. Write the verses onto two separate index cards as well, and/or add into your memory verses list.

_____

Pray that the Lord will protect you from the wrong kind of people, and that you remain mindful of God's great strength and power to protect you when other people appear strong. Ask God to help you see through His eyes.

_____

•　　•　　•　　•　　•　　•

Day 4

Obey

This one deals with your sisters and brothers. God commands us to "love one another" in John 15:12. Growing with God starts at home. No hitting, no name-calling, and no making them cry. Instead, be giving, loving, and encouraging. Put their needs first. Obey by loving your sisters and brothers. Be grateful for them. You have to admit, they are pretty funny, and a lot of times they are fun. This is obedience, and this is a great way to be closer to God, and grow into a Godly man. This is how you pave your path.

No siblings? Whom do you find yourself spending much of the day with, whether you want to or not? The girl that sits next to you in class? The neighbors? Your cousins? Your friends? The people that are around you during the day are giving you the opportunity to apply God's Word: love one another. Be grateful for them. Help them. Pray for them.

1 John 2:10 says, "He who loves his brother abides in the light, and there is no cause for stumbling in him."

Dear Heavenly Father, help me to love those around me. Help me to follow Jesus, especially when they make me angry. Help me to see them as You see them. In Jesus' name, Amen.

Lesson 3
Establish the Setting

Day 1

Soon to follow is a summary of chapters up to I Samuel 13. This is not a detour from reading up to I Samuel 13 yourself. Actually, you will have a better grip on understanding what is going on if you do take time to read these chapters. In these chapters, God shows His power through the ark, and these chapters list many of the towns and cities that we will be reading about. However, there is such an abundance of information and history in these chapters that the life of David would have to be completely booted out of this study and into another one. Since we are studying the life of David, we are simply establishing the setting with chapters 2 – 13.

I highly recommend you read these chapters *after* completing this study. They are super interesting and really good reading!

Chapters 2:27 – 15:34

The lives of Eli and his sons come to an end. The Philistines killed the sons, and Eli, brokenhearted, fell back, broke his neck, and died.

Samuel continues to grow with the Lord. His walk with God was so wonderful that the entire country of Israel knew Samuel's name. He was well-known as a distinguished man of God. Because Samuel devoted himself to God, it made a difference in all of Israel: "And the hand of the LORD was against the Philistines all the days of Samuel" (7:13).

During this time, Israel did not have kings to rule the country. They had a judge, and Samuel was that judge. The people in Israel told Samuel they did not want a judge. They wanted a king "like all the other nations." Feeling rejected, Samuel prayed. God was to always be the King of Israel. Samuel tried to explain this to the Israelites, but the Israelites felt they needed to be more like other countries who had a king. God was rejected, yet He answered to Samuel, "Give the people what they want. Appoint them a king."

God guided Samuel to appoint a man named Saul to be king. Saul *appeared* to love God, but he had a hard time growing with God. Saul often felt that his way of thinking was just as good as God's instructions. Samuel, a great man of God and the priest, explained to Saul in I Samuel 13:13,

"You have done foolishly. You have not kept the commandment of the LORD your God, which He commanded you. For now the LORD would have established your kingdom over Israel forever." (v.14) But now your kingdom shall not continue. The LORD has sought for Himself a man after His own heart."

A man after God's own heart was to be the next king. It was a young man actually. His name was David. The age of David was of no significance to God.

In our society, our age means quite a bit in terms of what we can and cannot do. For example, you are required to be a certain age to be employed for a job, and yet another age to drive a car, and another age to vote. However, in the eyes of our great God, your age is of no concern. God sees your heart. Is your heart seeking God? More importantly, is your heart seeking God's heart? Do you have a burning desire within you to know what God loves, what He hates, what brings Him joy, and what gives Him grief? It is in God's heart what makes Him

Read

Apply

Obey

Pray

smile, and what it is about YOU that makes Him lovingly gaze at you, longing to spend time with you forever and ever.

Have your eyes ever filled with tears because you know God's eyes are filled with tears, too? Have you ever danced and raised your hands in praise knowing that God is rejoicing with His angels?

Like David, who was just a boy like you, do you want to be a man after God's own heart? Write your thoughts:

Yes, because God's heart is the best heart.

Time and time again, the Bible gives us many young people who lived to know God's heart. Here are some examples:

★ *Samuel:* He was raised in the House of the Lord. Samuel heard God's voice at a young age (Check out I Samuel 3.)

★ *King Josiah:* He turned the people of Israel away from false idols and back to the laws and the will of God (2 Kings 22). He was 8 years old when he became king.

★ *Mary:* Mary may have been as young as 14 years of age when visited by the angel Gabriel.

★ *Jesus:* As a boy, He amazed the church leaders and elders.

★ *Timothy:* As a very young man, he became a preacher.

Pursuing God's heart takes courage. Indeed, being a man of God will give you a courageous heart. The next time someone asks you, "What do you want to be when you grow up?" try answering this way:

"When I grow up? Why wait?!!"

You are still growing, and you will always be surrounded with new things to learn. However, God does not expect you to wait until you are smarter and bigger to know His heart. He wants you to know all of Him now! Today is important! Today has a purpose!

LIVE IT!

Here is an encouraging verse from God to you that is just what you need to hear. Write **James 4:8** and memorize:

_____

_____

_____

LIVE IT!

One more....write **1 Timothy 4:12** and memorize:

_____

_____

_____

_____

_____

After you have memorized these verses, repeat the verses to three people. Also, write the verses on an index card or on your memory verses list.

_____

Close this Bible study asking God to help you see that He loves you so much, He already has a great plan for you starting today!

_____

The Way I See It...

by Christopher Foster

God called David "a man after His own heart." What an amazing statement from God! What did God see in David? God called David a man after His own heart long before we first meet David as a boy in the Bible. So what did God see in this boy?

Some might think that to receive an honor such as this, one would need to have very defining qualities such as power, riches, and fame. But, this was not the case for David, nor would it be for any of us. David was the opposite of power, riches, and fame, at least in the world's eyes. He was a little man, son of a shepherd, who had little if any money, and no fame to speak of.

However, he possessed character qualities that God must have seen as being honorable. God saw David's heart. God saw his thoughts of love for others, his actions of selflessness, his gratitude, and how he turned to God not only when times were rough, but even when times were good. God heard David sing praises to Him. God may have watched David's eager eyes as he heard and read scriptures of how God loved and provided for Moses, Noah, Abraham, and Israel. David was humble, selfless, serving, and a giving man who was determined to learn more about his great God. So he sought God. These are character qualities I and every man growing with God should work to attain.

God also sees and watches us. Walking with the Lord is a life-long process, and I continue to learn more about my Heavenly Father, and about the intricacies of God's plan for me each day. However, it is not about God's plan for me that I strive to find. It is God I strive to find and to know more and more. If I daily seek God, my life is joyful, and a joyful life is exactly what God wants you and me to have.

Lesson 4
Review

Read Psalm 119:24.

LIVE IT!

This is the key verse of this whole book. Write the verse out and memorize:

_____

_____

_____

_____

A counselor is someone who guides and instructs another to live wisely and joyfully. For example, Jesus is our Counselor (The prophet Isaiah knew He would be. See Isaiah 9:6.). Psalm 119:24 tells us why we read and study men and women in the Bible – through these people, God counsels us to know Him more, and on how we can live wisely and joyfully here on earth. God wants to guide and instruct you to be a responsible and godly young man.

Although we have just touched the surface into I Samuel, reflect on all that you have studied, including the memory verses, the Bible passages you have read, and how it all is applying to your life at this very moment.

Apply & Obey

Listed here is a review of what you have studied thus far:

1. **Be grateful to God.**

   > Psalm 113:3   *From the rising of the sun to its going down, the LORD'S name is to be praised.*

2. **Do not fear.**

   > Joshua 1:9   *Have I not commanded you? Be strong and of good courage; do not be afraid, nor be dismayed, for the LORD your God is with you wherever you go.*

   Read

   Apply

   and,

   Obey

   Pray

   > Psalm 91:11, 12   *For He shall give His angels charge over you, To keep you in all your ways. In their hands they shall bear you up, Lest you dash your foot against a stone.*

3. **You are never too young!**

   > James 4:8   *Draw near to God and He will draw near to you.*

   > 1 Timothy 4:12   *Let no one despise your youth, but be an example to the believers in word, in conduct, in love, in spirit, in faith, in purity.*

4. **Enjoy and learn from the counselors of the Bible.**

   > Psalm 119:24   *Your testimonies also are my delight and my counselors.*

Reflect on these six verses by thinking about each one. Make sure you have each verse memorized. They become your tools for life, and you will surely need them.

Do you remember to thank God for all and how much He blesses you?

Do you believe that God is stronger than your fears and your age?

Think very hard: what is the strongest person or thing that you know of in the world (be it a lion, an elephant, a shark, a boxer, the president....)?

_____

God is looking at what you just wrote down, and He is replying to you similarly to the way He replied to Job in Job 38 – 41: "Is this the strongest thing you can think of? That's tiny. By the way, it only came to be because I allowed it." Remember, He is with you and He is stronger than all your fears and doubts. Your fears and doubts feed Satan; your faith in God feeds your joy, and glorifies God. Now do not fear your fear. Pray. God is as forgiving as He is strong. That is a great blessing in your life.

_____

Pray thanksgiving to God for His strength and great love, and anything else that may be in your heart.

_____

Chapter 3

Day by Day

There is a reason for the meaningless things we do. Simple, boring tasks like feeding the dog, cleaning the toilets, waiting in line at a grocery store, or sitting by Great Grandma as she holds her teeth in her lap. Or maybe, like David, you have to watch sheep, and take lunch to your big brothers. Do not underestimate a single minute in your life. Always be ready to hear God and obey God. Start by praying and reading your Bible.

You are absolutely going to love reading the life of David! Before you start each study, pray to God. As you read your Bible, think about why God wants you to read each verse. How does a passage apply to your life? Which part really speaks to you? Always write your own summary and your thoughts of the reading.

Remember, you can refer to the map anytime you see the name of a place in your reading. Every city mentioned is on the map. Now that you are equipped with a map and background information, let us observe the early days of David.

Israel
1 Samuel 16 & 17

ARAMEANS

Sea of
Galilee

Mediterranean
Sea

*Ramah(16:13 – Samuel's home)

*Ekron (17:52)

*Jerusalem(17:54)

*Bethlehem(16:1)

Gath(17:52)*

* Azekah (17:1)

Dead

Philistine

*Shaaraim(17:52)

Sea

Territory

VALLEY OF ELAH

*Sochoh (17:1)

N

I-------I 10 miles

32

Lesson 1

The Heart

Day 1

Read I Samuel 16:1-13.

Explanations in your reading:

16:1 "Fill your horn with oil…." An animal's horn, such as a ram, was used as a container to hold oil. These essentials were needed to show God's will in someone's life. Anointing means to smear or to rub in. When one is anointed, God 'smears in' His truth and His will. The oil being poured over the head is a symbol of this gift from God.

Read

Apply

Obey

Pray

16:4 "And the elders trembled at his coming…" Samuel was very well known as a powerful man of God. His presence was known to make a difference. This made people nervous and excited.

16:5 "Sanctify yourselves…" This means to separate yourself from any sin in your surroundings, and any sin in your hearts and minds. Getting clean.

Write a summary and your own thoughts of the reading:

_____

_____

_____

_____

_____

•   •   •   •   •   •

Day 2

Apply & Obey

LIVE IT!

God taught Samuel a lesson in verse 7. Write down **I Samuel 16:7b** and memorize:

_____

_____

_____

_____

_____

Repeat the verse to three people. Write this verse on one of your index cards and/or your memory verses list.

Sometimes, we look at people and decide they are bad, or they are sinners, or they need improving in some way. Often, we make these decisions based on how they look...what we *see*. We might laugh at them, or shake our heads in disapproval.

LIVE IT!

Name one or more persons and/or times you have judged someone based on how he/she looked. Ask a parent if you need help.

_____

_____

_____

_____

_____

Now **read I Samuel 16:7** (above) again.

Then pray,

*"God, forgive me for judging others. Help me **now** to see those*

that I judge the way You see them. Help me see their hearts.

Dear God, what does their heart look like to You?"

When we look at others, we cannot see their hope, their fears, their shamefulness, their sadness, their anger, or their confusion. We cannot see what they have been through, or how their hearts may be breaking. We cannot see how they may be starving for the Truth and for love. We cannot see their confusion as they don't know where to reach for God's eternal love.

Or it may be that we cannot see how a person that looks undesirable could deeply love God. Maybe we do not see anything right away, not the way God does.

Everyone wants truth and love. Not just the good-looking people.

Write down how you think God viewed this person you listed above (remember, He sees the heart):

_____

_____

_____

_____

Pray and ask God to help you see this person the same way He sees them.

You cannot be a judgmental man after God's own heart.

That is an oxymoron,

like "run slowly," or "awfully good," or "definitely maybe," or "absolutely unsure," or "act natural," or "eat fast."

You cannot be a judgmental man after God's own heart.

Judge not!

• • • • • •

Day 3

One of the best ways for us to get to know David is by reading one of his Psalms.

LIVE IT!

Read Psalm 18:25-36. Underline or highlight verses you like.

_____

Before you close this book for the day, pray asking God to help you see the love He has for others, and pray to God about whatever you feel in your heart.

_____

The Way I See It...

by Christopher Foster

I was born with a cleft lip. This meant that I had a minor facial abnormality. In my very young years up until about five or six years old I never saw myself as being any different than anyone else. Once I started school, my peers let me know very quickly that I was different.

From then on through my adolescent years there would be many times that I was judged based on my appearance. During this time, I developed a very "thick skin," and I learned to be comfortable in the body God gave me.

I also believe it was during this time that God began to instill in me the importance of a servant's heart, and the importance of not judging others. God says in Romans 14:13, "Therefore let us not judge one another anymore, but rather resolve this, not to put a stumbling block or a cause to fall in our brother's way." This is much easier to understand as an adult than as a child, but having this verse close to my heart even at a young age helped to remind me of the importance of not doing something that can be so easy to do.

Lesson 2
This is the Day!

Verse 13 ends stating, "So Samuel arose and went to Ramah." Ramah was Samuel's home. He just had a big night, you know, anointing God's chosen and all. It was just not something Samuel did every day. So, he longed to be home.

Read I Samuel 16:14-23.

CHECK OUT THE MAP!

Explanations in your reading:

16:14   Saul rarely sought God, which created a distressing spirit from God to pour into Saul. Notice in Saul's sadness, he still did not seek God.

16:21   "…he became his armorbearer."

An armorbearer was a man hired to carry extra weapons or armor for someone else, particularly for a king. They were to help protect and to avenge their master's safety.

Write a summary and your own thoughts of the reading:

_____

_____

_____

_____

_____

• • • • • •

Day 2

Apply & Obey

Isn't this interesting? David got a new job. Quite a change from the day-by-day shepherding lifestyle! Keep in mind that King Saul has no idea yet that his harpist has also been anointed to one day sit in Saul's seat as king!

God has a plan, doesn't He? Everyday really does matter.

LIVE IT!

Write out, with as many details as possible, the schedule of what is left of your day. For example, add lunchtime, schoolwork, music practice, downtime, chores, go with Mom to grocery store,… whatever you can think of that will show what is left for you to do today:

_____

_____

_____

_____

_____

_____

_____

_____

_____

Now read David's God-inspired words in **Psalm 40:8.**

Where in your schedule can you greatly love the Lord, perhaps by praying, singing, sharing with siblings, helping and honoring your parents, being thankful, or sharing the gospel? On your day's schedule, squeeze in activities that show delight in God's will for your life.

For example, today I have to fold clothes. So I am going to squeeze in that I will listen to praise music or sing a praise song as I fold the clothes. Or I have to scrub the shower. So I will go over my memory verses in my head while I scrub the shower.

It is not that folding clothes and scrubbing the shower is not fruitful enough. I am still honoring God. However, by adding a little extra delight in God helps me remember that it is all worthwhile. It means something. It is a building block in God's will for our lives.

He has an amazing plan for you! Rejoice today in this truth!

Before you close this Bible study for the day, pray and ask God to help you see Him and His glory in everything you do today.

Lesson 3
Man, that's Heavy!

Day 1

Read 1 Samuel 17:1-11.

Explanations in your reading:

17:4   "...whose height was six cubits and a span."

That's 9 feet 6 inches tall. By the way, it's not the first time giants are mentioned in the Bible – see for yourself....

17:5   "...a coat of mail...the coat was five thousand shekels..."

A warrior's armor made out of chains of metal that overlap and look scaly is a coat of mail. Five thousand shekels equals about 78 pounds of weight.

17:7   "...staff of his spear was like a weaver's beam..."

Through these scriptures, God is showing you that this guy was super-big. Even his spear was abnormally large.

Write a summary and your own thoughts of the reading:

_____

_____

_____

_____

_____

• • • • • •

Day 2

Apply & Obey

Goliath was no small guy. His great size, without a doubt, encouraged him to presume he was powerful and in control. Goliath had a great deal of confidence. He was very bold to place himself in the middle of two fighting enemies, being the Philistine army and the Israelite army. He was so confident that he terrified all the men of Israel. Goliath just knew that there was no one as big and as bad as he. Goliath was probably having a great time and loving life just the way it was, being so big and mighty. Be that as it may, Goliath was without God, so Goliath fell.

Read

Apply

Obey

Pray

This still happens today. Many people with great strengths and talents live for themselves and not for God. Therefore, they always fall. God gave Goliath his great size and strength, but Goliath never gave anything back to God.

LIVE IT!

Think of your own strengths, and list them. Perhaps you can include strengths such as intelligent, friendly, a witness, handsome, inventive, entertaining, loving, funny, obedient, saved, honest, athletic, or musical. If any of these strengths describe you, or if you can think of others, add them to your list. If you are stuck, ask a parent/caretaker what your strengths are. Try to list at least three strengths (in the left column only):

_____   _____

_____   _____

_____   _____

_____   _____

_____   _____

Once your list is complete, first of all, remember these are all strengths that God has given you. Now, think of how you can use these strengths to serve God. Write your ideas beside each strength. For example, if you wrote "funny," you may choose to help someone who is sad or lonely laugh.

You are well aware that the more we use our muscles, the bigger they become. Your God-given strengths work the same way. Carry out these acts of serving God today. The more you use your strengths for God, the stronger they will become.

Pray and ask God to help you see and use your strengths
to love Him and others.

Lesson 4
Fathers Know Best

Day 1

Read   I Samuel 17:12-22.

Explanations in your reading:

> 17:17 "…an ephah of this dried grain…" An ephah is a bushel of grain.

Write a summary and your own thoughts of the reading:

_____

_____

_____

_____

_____

. . . . . .

Day 2

Apply & Obey

Now that another battle against the Philistines has begun, David goes home to be with his aging father Jesse, and tend to the sheep. When Jesse gave David an errand, David arose early to carry out his father's instructions.

David may have had the words of Exodus 20:12 in his heart. He did this because, as mentioned in 1 Samuel 13:14, "The LORD has sought for Himself a man after His own heart." David knew Scripture because he wanted to know God.

Write **Exodus 20:12** here, and memorize. Then share with at least three other people. Also, write this memory verse on one of your index cards or in your memory verses list.

_____

_____

_____

_____

In order for David to obey God, he had to start by obeying his earthly parents. In order for you to honor and obey God, you have to start at home by obeying your parents/caretakers. It is not always easy to obey and honor parents. Therefore, you must start practicing now. The better you get at it, the better you will be able to honor and obey God. By the way, here is a forewarning: it is not always easy to obey God either. Start practicing at home today!

_____

Pray now and ask God to help you obey and honor your parents. Ask God to help you see your disobedience and how ungodly it is.

_____

Lesson 5
"Down with the Reproach!"

Read I Samuel 17:23-39.

Explanations of your reading:

> 17:26 "...uncircumcised Philistine..." David was commenting on Goliath's separation from God being uncircumcised. David is basically calling Goliath an ungodly foreigner.

Write a summary and your own thoughts of the reading:

_____

_____

_____

_____

_____

• • • • • •

Day 2

Apply & Obey

Wow! This boy has guts! Let's look at why. First of all, think about what David did *not* do: David did not just drop off the supplies to the soldiers without greeting them and spending time with them. He did not stand silently on the sidelines to let others worry about Goliath. When King Saul told David in verse 33, "no way,"

46

David did not walk away with his head down. He was not shy, and he was not a coward.

Instead, here is what young David did and why:

#1 David walked onto the battlefield to say hello to, as he says, "the armies of the Living God." David wanted to fellowship with other believers.

Being with others who love the Lord will give us strength, and God will be there, too.

Read

Apply

Obey

Pray

Read **Psalm 133:1**, and write these God-inspired words of David here:

_____

_____

_____

_____

Memorize this verse, write it on an index card or in your memory verses list, and share this verse with three people.

It is my prayer that you fellowship with other believers in Jesus Christ. Take the time to greet others by *shaking hands*. Are you comfortable with shaking hands with others? If you are reading this Bible Study, you are old enough to be shaking hands.

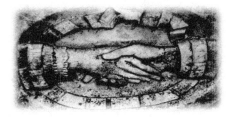

LIVE IT!

Here's a *challenge* for you (this will be fun):

Shake hands with at least 20 people in one week. Make eye contact, hold out your hand, and verbalize a greeting, such as, "Good to see you," "How are you,"

"Hello," "Good morning/afternoon," "Hi, my name is _____." You may want to tell as many people as you can, "I am learning to greet others as David did."

Do not wait for someone to hold out his hand to shake. You go first! When you start the shake, it will help you feel more comfortable, and it will help the other person feel accepted and cared for. Also, hand-shakes show friendship, brotherhood, and unity.

You will have to create a way to keep up with your hand-shake count. Once you have completed the challenge, write these words here, "I DID IT!"

_____

Then, keep on shakin'!

•　•　•　•　•　•

Day 3

#2 David was standing with the valiant men of Israel as Goliath "the Terrible" roared again, and he had no fear. All the men trembled with fear, all but David.

Because of David's strong relationship with God, he immediately viewed Goliath as God did – weak, because Goliath was without God. David's strong faith glowed, even though ridiculed by Eliab, his brother.
David turned heads, meaning he had such great character and courage many men noticed him. This great character and courage came from having a relationship with God. David was even talked about to the king, and the king wanted to see him.

Write down these God-inspired words of David from **Psalm 27:1**. Memorize the verse, write it on your index cards and/or your memory verses list, and share with three people:

_____

_____

_____

_____

_____

_____

These words may have been singing in David's heart while Goliath was shouting.

LIVE IT!

Place this verse where you can see it many times every day. Tape it to your bathroom mirror, or in your bedroom,   on the refrigerator, or any place you can think of. If you will hide these words in your heart, repeating them many times every day, your strength in the Lord and your courage by the Lord will grow.

Important words to OBEY

God repeatedly tells us in the Bible to not fear. This does not mean you should fearlessly pick up snakes or run out into a busy street. That is not called having no fear. That is called having no sense. Instead, God wants us to fear Him. Understand, with the mind God gave you, that we are to obey His word, or *fear* the consequences.

_____

Pray and thank God for the people around you that help you grow closer to Him.
Thank God for each person by name. These people
in your life are a great blessing from God.

_____

Lesson 6
Review

Both Books of Samuel are among my personal favorites. The whole Goliath ordeal is coming up and is exciting, but this is just one of many exciting adventures of growing closer to God.

Listed here is a review of what you have studied thus far:

1. **Do not judge others.**

   1 Samuel 16:7   "For the LORD does not see as man sees; for man looks at the outward appearance, but the LORD looks at the heart."

   Read

   Apply

   Obey

   Pray

2. **Love Mom and Dad.**

   Exodus 20:12   Honor your father and your mother, that your days may be long upon the land which the LORD your God has given you.

3. **Fellowship.**

   Psalm 133:1   Behold, how good and how pleasant it is for brethren to dwell together in unity!

4. **Do not fear (yes, again).**

   Psalm 27:1   The LORD is my light and my salvation; whom shall I fear? The LORD is the strength of my life; of whom shall I be afraid?

Rememorize all the above verses, and share the verses with others. Then, think about and meditate on these instructions: *do not fear; do not judge others; love mom and dad; and fellowship.* Think about how difficult or easy each one is.

Precious brother in Christ, don't grow weary!   All must be made part of our lives to grow with God, but choose three instructions that you would like to concentrate the most on for the next few days.

List them here:

_____

_____

_____

Share this with a parent or a spiritual leader. Ask them to pray for you.

Write out your own prayer:

_____

_____

_____

_____

_____

_____

_____

_____

_____

_____

Thank God for His constant flow of HIS love in your life.

Thank Him for His Holy Spirit that guides you closer to HIM.

_____

The Way I See It...

by Christopher Foster

David killing Goliath is the ultimate story of the little man taking out the big, bad bully. However, it is also the story that can symbolize the many "Goliaths" that we may face throughout our lives, and these "Goliaths may not always be big and bad bully's!

For the sake of this commentary, I'll say the "Goliaths" are everyday trials that we may face. I have days where I feel like my trials are nine feet tall, and impossible to overcome. David, as small as he was, had the confidence of a giant twice as big as Goliath when he went up against his foe.

Where did he get his confidence to overcome this giant of a trial? The same place that I get mine, the Lord God! It's amazing that thousands of years ago, David pulled from the same source when going into trials that I do today.

Chapter 4

The Really Real World

It is time for David to see more of the world than he probably ever wanted to see. My dear, sweet brother in Christ, you will (if you haven't already) see more of the world than you ever want to see as well. By God's love and grace and by your obedience, you will be prepared. David's obedience to God is now a gift to you in the Bible.

Love your Bible. Always hold on to it, and all that God says to you. It is the ONLY place you can go to know the real world.

Enjoy using your map as you follow along with all David's travels.

Israel
1 Samuel 17:52 – 22:23

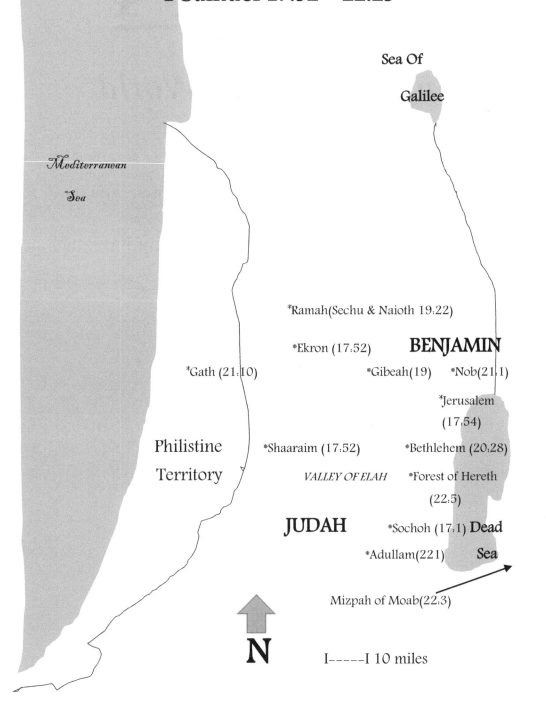

Sea Of

Galilee

Mediterranean

Sea

*Ramah(Sechu & Naioth 19:22)

*Ekron (17:52)   **BENJAMIN**

*Gath (21:10)   *Gibeah(19)   *Nob(21:1)

*Jerusalem

(17:54)

Philistine   *Shaaraim (17:52)   *Bethlehem (20:28)

Territory   *VALLEY OF ELAH*   *Forest of Hereth

(22:5)

JUDAH   *Sochoh (17:1) **Dead**

*Adullam(221)   **Sea**

Mizpah of Moab(22:3)

N

I-----I 10 miles

Lesson 1
Off with his Head!

Day 1

Read I Samuel 17:40-58.

Explanations of the reading:

v. 41 "the man who bore the shield went before him."

Goliath actually had a soldier walk in front of him carrying a shield...was this really necessary??

Write a summary and your own thoughts of the reading:

_____

_____

_____

_____

_____

Reading the Bible can be so much fun! . . . YES! David cut off Goliath's head! Wow! It's not a popular picture shown in a children's Sunday school class. You probably never had a coloring sheet showing David cutting off Goliath's head. You may not even be allowed to watch movies this gruesome! God knows how to entertain you like no one else!

• • • • • •

Day 2

David actually had more weapons for battle than Goliath. Sure, David had his sling and his stones, but he also had the whole armor of God, as written in Ephesians 6:13-20.

LIVE IT!

Read Ephesians 6:13-20, then fill in the blanks:

1. His waist was girded with _____.

2. He had the breast plate of _____.

3. His feet were prepared with the gospel of

   _____.

4. He had the shield of _____.

5. He had the helmet of _____.

6. He had the sword of the _____,

   which is _____.

Truth should be wrapped around us like belt. It represents purity. *Righteousness* is like a breastplate covering our heart. When we choose to do what is right, our hearts our moving toward God Almighty. The *gospel of peace* at our feet means that we approach others with a loving, friendly heart, not hateful or judgmental. Our *faith* is like a shield that protects us and keeps fear away, because we know our God is strong and is with us. Our *salvation* shelters our entire head. It is in our head that we know Jesus Christ, God's Son, took our sins and we will live eternally with Him. The *Holy Spirit* gives us so much strength as if we have a sword in our hand ready for war against sin.

Read

Apply

Obey

Pray

LIVE IT!

Take a look at each of the following strengths. Rate each strength, from 1 to 6, with 1 being the strength that you believe is your strongest strength, 2 being your second strongest strength, 3 being your third strongest, and so on:

_____   Truth (honesty)

_____   Righteousness (choosing to do what is right)

_____   Gospel of peace (loving toward others, not argumentative)

_____   Faith (trusting God by praying and reading the Bible)

_____   Salvation (believing that your sin is forgiven through Jesus)

_____   Holy Spirit (submitting to His work in your life)

Which one do you believe you have been gifted with by God?

_____

Name a time in your life when you were strong with this gift:

_____

_____

_____

Which strength do you believe is the weakest (or rather, not as strong)?

_____

Can you think of a time when you were not wearing this part of your "armor"?

_____

_____

_____

_____

You may have been guided by the Holy Spirit to write a "6" beside the strength you chose as the weakest. Even if you wrote a 6 beside Holy Spirit, maybe He wants you to listen, obey, and walk closer to Him.

Whichever one you wrote a 6 beside, pray about it. Thank God for showing you! Think about it, but *do not* worry about it.

If you do not know your weaknesses, you cannot make them stronger!

Now you know, and God has shown you. Only God can strengthen you. Ask Him, just as David did in **Psalm 139:23, 24:**

v.23 Search me, O God, and know my heart; Try me and know my anxieties;

v.24 And see if there is any wicked way in me, and lead me into the way of everlasting.

Amen!

• • • • • •

Days 4 & 5

LIVE IT!

Reflect on **Ephesians 6:13-20**. Write it out, and memorize. Please, sweet brother in Christ, do not grow weary in writing this scripture. You may split the copy work up into two days.

_____

_____

_____

_____

_____

_____

_____

_____

_____

_____

_____

_____

_____

_____

_____

_____

_____

_____

_____

_____

_____

_____

In prayer, thank God for His word and His strength. Thank Him for showing you and guiding you closer to Him, and pray about all that is in your heart.

Lesson 2
Pick Me...Last

Day 1

Read I Samuel 18: 1 – 9.

Explanations in your reading:

v. 1   ". . . the soul of Jonathan was knit . . ." They became best friends, under the love and will of God. Jonathan will later play an important role in David's safety.

v. 2   "Saul . . . would not let him go home. . ." As King, Saul had the right to appoint anyone   at any time to do anything. Take a look at 1 Samuel 8:11 – 17.

v. 3   ". . . took off the robe that was on him. . ." Jonathan is King Saul's son, which means he is a prince, which means he is next in line to be king. His robe is of royalty and showed his rightful entitlement to the throne. Jonathan willingly gives his privilege of Kingship to David by giving him the robe of an heir. Jonathan shows that he prefers God's will over being next in line to be king.

v. 7   "Saul has slain his thousands, and David has slain his ten thousands." The women in the town are not praising Saul and David. They are making fun of King Saul.

Write a summary and your own thoughts of the reading:

Read

Apply

Obey

Pray

_____

_____

_____

_____

_____

_____

_____

• • • • • •

Day 2

These verses show a big difference between King Saul and Jonathan. One *wants* attention for *his* will. One *gives up* attention for *God's* will.

The words of the singing women offended King Saul, and rightly so. However, Saul took that offense into the wrong way of thinking: "David's trying to overthrow my kingdom! That sneaky David!"

To put more fuel on the fire (so to speak), David becomes best friends with King Saul's son Jonathan, AND David excels in wisdom, AND David is loved by all around the kingdom. Now, instead of loving David also and feeling blessed to have David working in his kingdom, Saul's teeth cringe at David's success. Oh, this just might get ugly. . .

Apply & Obey

It is simple: Saul sought the approval of men and ends up in grief – David sought to bring only God glory and is loved by all. It is nice to be loved, to be noticed, and to be chosen. Everyone wants that. Even the shy introvert must admit that being noticed for a strength or an accomplishment feels great, as it should.

There is absolutely nothing wrong with winning the approval of others. However, there are two big problems with *seeking* approval from others.

First of all, it is temporary; it will not last. The approval and praise you receive from others are usually based on what you *do*, not who you *are*. Your family, a small group of people that know you, and maybe one or two close friends are more than likely the only people on earth right now that love you for who you are, no matter what you do! Also, these are the few people in your life that will forever love you. Their love for you, (like God's) is not temporary, it is eternal.

The other problem with seeking approval from others is that the approval is given by sinners. We are all sinners, right? The Bible tells us so in Romans 3:23. Many times, we (sinners) give our approval to someone based on what they can do or have done for us. This is not a bad thing. We should admire those who help us fix our bike, or that will take the time to play ball with us, or those who give us candy, or give us encouragement. Therefore, it is a fleshly praise. The praise you receive is again based on what you *do*, not who you *are*.

Do not *seek* approval from others. There is a better praise to seek that far outweighs any admiration we can get from a person.

> Seeking to bring our Heavenly Father joy compares to absolutely nothing else you can do. Please remember that God does not deeply love you because of the great things you do. God already loves you completely, from your hair to your toenails, exactly the way you are and exactly who you are. You cannot win God's love. He loved you first!

Here's a question: so if God already loved David, why did David bother trying to please God? He could have stood behind God's army and let the Israelites take care of the Philistines and Goliath. God would still love David. He could have chosen a simpler life.

Here's the thing: David would be no closer to God's heart. We seek to bring God glory in our actions because we love Him. When we have a relationship with God, we will love Him more. Consequently, we will *want* to bring Him glory. We do what is good for GOD.

When you bring God glory, you will experience amazing joy. Then, others may love you and praise you – others may hate you and reject you; but brother, you've got joy!

LIVE IT!

How do you want to bring God glory? How do you believe the Holy Spirit is working in you to bring God glory? You may be thinking of today, tomorrow, and days ahead. But write down how you feel you would love to bring God glory and grow closer to His heart:

_____

_____

_____

Write down and memorize **Psalm 115:1**.

_____

_____

_____

_____

_____

_____

Once you have memorized the verse, repeat it to three people. Remember to write the verse on an index card and/or your memory verses list.

_____

Use this verse, Psalm 115:1, in your prayer time.
Repeat these words to your loving Heavenly Father now.
Ask God to help you see His love.

_____

The Way I See It...

As a Christian man, I am to seek God daily. The Lord wants me to seek Him daily. It is clear to me that when I do this, decisions are made easier and challenges are more manageable. I have confidence knowing that I have His support when I seek Him. Consequently, I have found that I do not feel as confident when I try to seek others and not God. The advice of others, the support of others, encouragement and praise from others are nice, but it's not the same. Don't worry about getting praise from others. **HOWEVER***, that does not mean you do not need to care what others think. Outside observations and guidance is a blessing from God we must, in humility, take.*

Proverbs 1:7 states "The fear of the LORD is the beginning of knowledge. But fools despise wisdom and instruction." Seeking God and not men also does not mean we are not to care for others and love others. We tend to think that if someone can help us none, we have no use for them. That is a selfish way of thinking. We love and care for others because God's love compels us to love and care. We do not love and care for others because we get a cookie out of the deal. Jesus comments in Matthew 5 that even the pagans do that! Just seek God daily.

Lesson 3
The Power of Love

Day 1

Read I Samuel 18:10-30.

Explanations in your reading:

v. 10 "… and he prophesied inside the house."

To prophesy can mean to preach, or to speak in tongues, or to become completely aware of God's plan and God's will and profess it. Here, Saul may have been hit smack in the face (figuratively speaking) with God's plan, and he may realize that his kingdom will not last.

v. 17 "Let my hand not be against him…"

Saul plans for David to be killed in battle by the Philistines. Then, Saul feels he will not be guilty of murder.

v.25 "…one hundred foreskins of the Philistines."

This is the cost David must pay in order to marry Saul's daughter Mi'chal. In other words, Saul is saying, "Kill one hundred Philistines as a 'thank you' for my daughter." Saul assumes David will be killed by one Philistine before David kills 100 Philistines.

David twice exclaims to King Saul, "I am not worthy to marry your daughter."

Does David know Saul wants him dead? Possibly. Does David revere Saul as a worthy King? Yes, completely.

Write a summary and your own thoughts of the reading:

_____

_____

_____

_____

_____

. . . . . .

Day 2

Apply & Obey

Read

Apply

Obey

Pray

It is really difficult to love people who hurt us. When we are called names, laughed at, hit, spoken to hatefully, or just ignored, love seems to dwindle, and pride swells. It seems to make us feel better to judge those that hurt us, but it helps nothing.

Judging only plants a seed of hate in our hearts. **1 John 4:7, 8** must be rooted in your heart:

> **Beloved, let us love one another, for love is of God; and everyone who loves is born of God and knows God. (v.8) He who does not love does not know God, for God is love.**

This verse might just be a life-saver for you. It has been for many, and it was for David.

LIVE IT!

Copy this verse **(1 John 4:7, 8)**, and memorize:

_____

_____

_____

_____

_____

Repeat this verse to three people, and add to your index cards and/or memory verses list.

• • • • • •

Day 3

David never judged or hated Saul, even after Saul tried to kill him. David considered others better than himself.

Read the verse above again.

Did David know God? _____

Did David love Saul? _____

How is it that David knew God?

_____

_____

_____

Whom in your life have you hated or judged?

_____

_____

Now, write down these words of **Matthew 5:43, 44** of our Savior Jesus:

_____

_____

70

_____

_____

_____

_____

_____

Memorize this passage, share it with three people, and add it to your index cards and/or memory verses list.

_____

Ask God to help you obey all that Jesus commands in Matthew 5:43– 48.

_____

Lesson 4
There's no Place Like Church!

Day 1

Read I Samuel 19:1 – 24.

Explanations in your reading:

v.18   Ramah and Nai'oth you will find
on your map.

Write a summary and your own thoughts of the reading:

_____

_____

_____

_____

_____

All of the car chases or "good guy/bad guy" movies you have ever seen are nothing compared to this! What's more, it's all true!

• • • • • •

Day 2

Apply & Obey

David fled to the home of God's anointed prophet Samuel. Perhaps David had Psalm 145:18 on his mind as he ran to Samuel's hometown Ramah.

Psalm 145:18

The LORD is near to all who call upon Him, to all who call upon Him in truth.

This verse feels like a warm blanket put around us by God. David knew he could rest in the presence of God with Samuel. They both loved God, and they both knew they needed Him.

Christian fellowship is powerful! It is nice to be with others who share your faith, who share what is in each other's hearts. Christian fellowship is also fun. It is a constant celebration where we can be immersed with the joy that we have victory in Jesus!

This is one reason why we go to church. We are there to be with each other and exalt God. It is where His presence feels so powerful! He reminds us that He is our Protector. When we leave, many times it feels like our heart has been cleaned out.

Also at church, we can meet others that want to know God's heart. It is where we express brotherly love, and rest in knowing God is always with us. There's no place like church!

Do you belong to a church that proclaims Jesus to be God's Son and our Savior? Are you in a youth group that powerfully proclaims their love for Jesus Christ? If yes, Amen! Go there and keep growing with God and others.

LIVE IT!

If you are not in a church or youth group, or you do not belong to a group of believers that regularly meet to proclaim God's word, you need to find one. Here are some ideas:

- Talk to your parents. Will they do one of three things: take you, go with you, or allow you to go with someone else?
- If you plan to go with someone other than a family member, scope out your options: where do the neighbors go to church? Where do some friends from school go to church? Are there Christians from your ball team, or another group that go to a church you would like to visit? How about other relatives – aunts, uncles, cousins, or grandparents?
- If you cannot find a secure weekly ride to church (however, you most likely will), call a church that you would like to attend and inform them

that you need a ride to their church. They will be honored that you called and asked for help, and you will definitely have a way to and from church.

Write and memorize these God-inspired words of David from **Psalm 84:10a** (first sentence only):

_____

_____

_____

_____

After memorizing this verse, share it with three people, and add the verse to your index cards and/or memory verses list.

●　　●　　●　　●　　●　　●

Day 3

David's life was to forever change. No more quiet time as a shepherd. No more joyful mornings with his dad. No more fun times with his big brothers. His daily, normal routine life was over. At this point, the thoughts that fill young David's mind are of his life and his death.

Read Psalm 7 to understand what kinds of thoughts and feelings David had. He really shares his heart in this chapter. How does it speak to your heart? Underline verses along the way that you like, that you want to memorize, or that speak to your heart. Add your own thoughts if you would like:

_____

_____

_____

Pray and thank God for His church where you can practically
see His greatness and glory. Pray for your church or another church.
Pray for the spiritual leaders of the church.

Lesson 5
Friends Forever!

Day 1

Read I Samuel 20.

Explanations in your reading:

> v. 5   "...New Moon..."   The beginning of first fruits of the month. A religious practice of regarding and revering God through sacrifices.

Write a summary and your own thoughts of the reading: ( )

_____

_____

_____

_____

• • • • • •

Day 2

Strategizing, scheming, and plotting secretively with a friend makes some of the best times together! However, Jonathan and David were not just passing time to be amusing, although they probably did have a tiny bit of a good time being quite sneaky! They strategized on how to escape the vengeful hands of King Saul by how arrows were shot.

Read

Apply

Obey

Pray

Their plan was quite clever: A time was set for Jonathan to shoot his bow as David hid far in the field. A young boy was instructed to go into the field and collect the

76

arrows as Jonathan shot them. If Jonathan's arrows fell beside the boy, this would be a sign to David that David was safe. If the arrows shot behind the boy, this was a sign to David that he was in danger against King Saul. Obviously, Jonathan was skilled in archery.

Apply & Obey

Jonathan sacrificed so much to help out his friend. He sacrificed his relationship with his father, his royal heritage, and he sacrificed his own life. Jonathan could have said, "Look, David. This is a big celebration that I will be attending. After I have my fun, we'll talk."

If we are friendly only at our convenience, does it constitute true friendship? More importantly, is it Christ-like? Sacrificing ourselves and our time is not easy, but the more you practice at it and make a conscious effort to stop your own plans for a moment, showing true love to your friends will become part of your heart and who you are.

To be a good friend or to have a good friend both require **three** ingredients:

1. A hunger to know God
2. Obeying God
3. Being good to each other for God.

LIVE IT!

To whom can you be a good friend (include more than one person, and hopefully, you are including siblings)?

_____

_____

Now, let's dive in more. Carefully read and consider the following fifteen ways to show love and gratitude to your friends. Choose at least **7** from the list to complete:

1. Call your friend on the phone, and tell him a funny joke.
2. Invite your friend to your house. Prepare (perhaps a list of) fun things to do.
3. Pray daily for your friend.
4. Buy a small gift for your friend with your own money (gum, candy, small toy).
5. Invite a friend on a family outing.
6. Invite a friend to go to church with you.
7. Ask your friend how you can pray for him.
8. Thank your friend for being a good friend.
9. Share what you have learned from this Bible study with your friend.
10. Plan a super-fun day or weekend with your friend.
11. Remember your friend's birthday.
12. If something tragic happens in your friend's life, visit him and let him know he can depend on you and trust you.
13. With your friend, think of a challenge that the both of you (or all of you) together would like to accomplish: running a race, swimming, target shooting, archery, any sport, juggling, writing/playing music, or anything you can think of that sounds like fun to learn. Schedule a date to get started.
14. Share how your relationship with God is going with your friend, and ask about how his relationship with God is going. It may be that you both have the same questions or thoughts, and you can help each other grow with God.
15. With your friend, take part in a ministry within the community: work together at a soup kitchen, do lawn work for an elderly person for no money, visit someone in a nursing home or in the hospital together, work in the church nursery together, pick up trash in a local park, share the gospel of Christ to children at a playground and/or other places you go, ask your pastor how you can care for others in your church.
16. Can you think of another way to be a great friend?

———————————————————————————————
———————————————————————————————
———————————————————————————————

Plan these activities on a calendar with your parents. Include more than one friend. These friendly acts may be spread out for a whole month, considering many things on the list depend on your parents' schedules.

•   •   •   •   •   •

Remember, true friends will love you based on who you are, not on the good things you do for them. Just the same, you must love your friends not by the good things they do for you, but for being your brother in Christ. Sound familiar? . . . **Ephesians 2:8** proclaims,

"For by grace you have been saved through faith, and that not of yourselves, it is a gift of God."

God loves us just the way He created us, not by the great things *we* have done. We are to reflect this love with our friends.

When anger or disappointment comes between you and your friend, do not walk away from the friendship. If this is your brother in Jesus Christ, repair the scratched or broken parts of the friendship, and continue to love and edify one another.

LIVE IT!

Look up the term **edify**, and write the definition here:

_____

_____

_____

Write **Ephesians 2:8** here, and memorize:

_____

_____

_____

_____

Once you have memorized this verse, share it with 3 other people, and add the verse to an index card.

---

*Pray for your friends, and thank God for showing you
in His word the beauty of Godly friendship.*

The Way I See It...

by Christopher Foster

In I Samuel 20, Jonathan proves to David that he is a true friend. I believe qualities of a true friendship include encouragement, support, selflessness, and trust. These ingredients have to be even stronger when times are rough.

In all honesty, true friendships will more than likely be few and far between as you grow. Thinking back, I can recall one friendship that I would call true and selfless. In high school, Chris and I were very similar. We were about the same size, made similar grades, liked girls, were both being raised in a Christian home, and we had the same cool name.

One hot summer day following graduation, Chris, myself, and two other friends were out enjoying the day, which unfortunately ended in a very bad car accident. I was thrown from the car, knocked unconscious. We were all scared, and we were all injured, but none as severe as my friend Chris. Chris had broken his neck in the accident. Only by the power of God did he survive. He would require a long hospital stay, and once at home he would have to wear a "HALO" brace for several months. This brace kept him from moving his shoulders, neck, and *head. During this time, he would not leave home, and his mobility was severely limited. The other three of us recovered from our injuries much more quickly, but in my heart I still felt the injuries of my friend Chris. I committed myself to spending time with him while he was healing. Although this was a rough time in our lives, our support and encouragement of each other only strengthened our friendship. I can genuinely say that Chris is a true friend. In I Samuel 20, Jonathan and David had a friendship similar to this. There was support for each other. They had the right ingredients: selflessness, encouragement, and trust.*

Lesson 6
Keep It Real True

Day 1

READ I Samuel 21:1 – 15.

CHECK OUT THE MAP!

Explanations in your reading:

v. 1   "Why are you alone?" Ahimelech noticed something was wrong considering David, who worked in the kingdom and was admired by all, was travelling alone.

v.4   "…no common bread…only holy bread…" Common bread was for all. Holy bread was set aside for priests.

v. 10   " …and went to Achish…" Achish was the king of Gath. David dared to go into Philistine territory!

Write a summary of the reading and your own thoughts:

_____

_____

_____

_____

• • • • • •

Day 2

At the beginning of Chapter 21, David is running for his life. Wherever he may go, be it home to Bethlehem, or the prophet Samuel, men of Saul will likely be there, waiting to kill David. So he flees to another man of God, Ahimelech.

Read

Apply

Obey

Pray

82

Good for David for seeking Godly fellowship, but this is as far as David's good deeds go… something seems to go terribly wrong.

David lies to the priest. David is dishonest! In his fear, his faith in God weakens, and so does his courage. So, he lies.

Then, things get stranger. David looks for safety with the Philistines. Yikes! When he realizes they are threatened by him, he pretends to be a crazy man!

Apply & Obey

The only man to walk the earth without sin was Jesus, not David. Therefore, David was a sinner. The first sin we are shown by David in God's Word is lying (bearing false witness). It is an ugly sin that poisons a liar's heart. There are *always* consequences to lying, even for David, as you will soon read.

There are two choices in front of you before you lie: the choice to let a lie protect you, or the choice to let God protect you. It is God, or it is the lie. It is honesty, or it is no God. It just sounds awful, doesn't it? Well, it is. There is just no way to sugar-coat it.

David's heart felt so heavy. Read **Psalm 120** to get an idea of how David felt.

LIVE IT!

Write out **Psalm 120:2**, and memorize it.

_____

_____

_____

_____

Repeat the verse to three people and add to your index cards and/or memory verses list.

• • • • • •

Day 3

Take your time answering these questions, and think about each one:

Why is it a relief that God knows we are not perfect?

_____

_____

_____

What if Romans 3:23 read, "Almost all are perfect and have not fallen short of the glory of God," and *you* are *not* one of those "almost alls." How would that effect your relationship with God?

_____

_____

_____

_____

David sinned at a time of massive emotions. He was feeling hurt, betrayed, depressed, and scared for his life.

LIVE IT!

Think about some of your own previous sins. What kinds of emotions were you feeling at the times of your sins?

_____

_____

Do you understand that these emotions that you felt may come again in your life? _____

Can you now pray and make a commitment to control your emotions?

_____

After praying, take a look at the proclamation on the next page. This is for you to fill in the blanks, and then present it to your parents. Insert your name in the first blank below. In the second blank, insert some emotions you have had when sinning. Read it to yourself completely. Keep the proclamation in the book, and allow a parent to make a copy if they would like. If you are ready to ask your parents to help hold you accountable to this request, sign at the bottom, and repeat the following to a parent:

"I,

_____,

confess that I have sinned at emotional times in my life. These emotions include

_____

_____.

When you see these emotions in me, remind me to put off my old self and to be renewed in the righteousness and holiness of God. Pray for me and help me to walk worthy of the calling with which God has called me. Thank you for helping me grow into a man of God. "

_____

Your signature

85

• • • • • •

Day 4

It is usually at an emotional time when we choose to sin. It is our flesh.

Read Romans 7:15 -8:1.

Why was it hard for Paul to stop sinning?

_____

_____

_____

_____

Read

Apply

Obey

Pray

Do you call Jesus your Savior? What does it mean that Jesus saves us from our sins?

_____

_____

_____

_____

_____

Write the definition of **condemnation**:

_____

_____

_____

Now write and memorize **Romans 8:1.**

_____

_____

_____

_____

_____

Share this verse with three people, and add to your index cards and/or your memory verses list.

God shows us in 1 Samuel 21 that even the man after His own heart made bad decisions sometimes. God forgave David, and He forgives you.

When we sin, we need to ask forgiveness, dust ourselves off, and keep reaching for our loving God!

_____

Thank God for his patience and forgiveness.
Ask God to help you stay completely honest.

_____

Lesson 7
Family Ties

Day 1

READ I Samuel 22.

CHECK OUT THE MAP!

Explanations in your reading:

v. 3   This is David loving, caring for, and protecting his parents.
        Also, refer to the map and look at the distance between Adullam
        to Mizpah of Moab.

v. 7   "Will the son of Jesse give…" Saul's point that he is trying to
        make is, "I can give you so much. David cannot give you
        anything!"

v. 18   "…a linen ephod…" This is clothing worn by priests. It is worn
        over clothes, similar to a smock or an apron. It signifies great
        reverence to God.

v. 22   "I have caused the death…" David realizes that his dishonesty
        with Ahimelech started this. If David was honest, things could
        have possibly been a lot different.

Write a summary of your reading and your own thoughts:

_____

_____

_____

_____

_____

_____

. . . . . .

Day 2

Apply & Obey

While David is hiding from Saul, about 400 friends and family members come to join him. 400! Yes, 400! Now, that's love! Not to mention, that is a great blessing from God!

Family is important. God gave you your family for strength, love, protection, fun, and to learn. Your family is your roots – you cannot grow without roots! You abide with them – you live with them; and surely you love them.

By abiding with and loving your family, you learn what it means to abide in and love Jesus. Your growth as a Christian man starts with your love for your family. This takes responsibility on your part.

God gave each family member roles, or responsibilities. You may share some roles with others in the family, such as caring for pets, or loving your siblings, or obeying your parents. Then there are some roles in which only you are responsible.

For example, if you are an *older* sibling, you have one of the biggest roles of the family. You must show your younger siblings how to live for Jesus. You must encourage your younger sibling(s) and love them. You must be patient, forgiving, and understanding that they (like you) are still learning. This is your role. It is no mistake that you were born first. God orchestrated your life this way. If you are an older brother, answer this question: How can being an older brother draw you closer to God?

_____

_____

_____

If you are a *younger* brother, like David, you also have distinct roles. First of all, you must be patient. Do not be in a hurry to grow up. Continually pray. Quietly watch others that are older, and learn. You must be a helper. Choose to love your older siblings, be thankful for them, and pray for them. You may be smaller, but you are not any less important to God. He loves the small and humble.

If you are a younger brother, answer this question: How can being a younger brother draw you closer to God?

_____

_____

_____

If you are the *only* child, then you are the oldest and the youngest, and God orchestrated your life this way. You have a unique opportunity to grow closer to Jesus like no one with siblings can. You may have many responsibilities for helping your parents. Unless parents help, it is up to you to get many things done. You do it yourself, you learn it yourself, and you complete it yourself. Help out cheerfully and confidently. Challenge yourself: can *you* cut the grass, try and fix something that is broken, wash the clothes, clean the kitchen, help fix the car? There are no siblings, so there is time to reach out to others, including neighbors, cousins, grandparents, other students at school, and teammates. Being the only child never means being lonely, and always means more responsibility.

If you are the only child, answer this question: How can being the only child in the house draw you closer to God?

_____

_____

_____

LIVE IT!

List five reasons why you are thankful for your family. Take a moment to pray and ask God to guide you in answering.

1. _____

2. _____

3. _____

4. _____

5. _____

Now list five ways you will try to do your part and strengthen your roles so that you are a strength to your family. Ask God, parents, and siblings for ideas.

1. _____

2. _____

3. _____

4. _____

5. _____

Write and memorize **Psalm 22:22.**

_____

_____

_____

_____

_____

After you have memorized the verse, share the verse with three people, and add to your index cards and/or memory verses list.

Remember, it is for our God that we love one another.

_____

Pray thanking God for your family,
and ask God to help you be a responsible family member
so that you will grow closer to God.

_____

Lesson 8
Keep in Mind

These last few days, you have completed some great reading! You are getting glimpses of the heart of God, and you are prayerfully beginning to see how God sees you, and His will for your life. Walking closer to God has so much to do with memorizing verses. In this chapter, you have had tons of verses to memorize. With every word you memorize, it is a step closer to God.

LIVE IT!

Following are all your verses from this chapter that you have memorized. Memorize them again. It should not be hard; just refresh your memory. Then, share all these verses with someone who is very important to you.

Ephesians 6:13-20
Therefore take up the whole armor of God, that you may be able to withstand in the evil day, and having done all, to stand. ¹⁴ Stand therefore, having girded your waist with truth, having put on the breastplate of righteousness, ¹⁵ and having shod your feet with the preparation of the gospel of peace; ¹⁶ above all, taking the shield of faith with which you will be able to quench all the fiery darts of the wicked one. ¹⁷ And take the helmet of salvation, and the sword of the Spirit, which is the word of God; ¹⁸ praying always with all prayer and supplication in the Spirit, being watchful to this end with all perseverance and supplication for all the saints— ¹⁹ and for me, that utterance may be given to me, that I may open my mouth boldly to make known the mystery of the gospel, ²⁰ for which I am an ambassador in chains; that in it I may speak boldly, as I ought to speak.

Psalm 115:1
Not unto us, O LORD, not unto us,
But to Your name give glory,
Because of Your mercy,
Because of Your truth.

1 John 4:7, 8
Beloved, let us love one another, for love is of God; and everyone who loves is born of God and knows God. He who does not love does not know God, for God is love.

Matthew 5:43, 44
"You have heard that it was said, 'You shall love your neighbor and hate your enemy.' [44] But I say to you, love your enemies, bless those who curse you, do good to those who hate you, and pray for those who spitefully use you and persecute you."

> *Read*
>
> *Apply*
>
> *Obey*
>
> *Pray*

Psalm 84:10
For a day in Your courts *is* better than a thousand.

Ephesians 2:8
For by grace you have been saved through faith, and that not of yourselves; *it is* the gift of God.

Psalm 120:2
Deliver my soul, O LORD, from lying lips
And from a deceitful tongue.

Romans 8:1
There is therefore now no condemnation to those who are in Christ Jesus, who do not walk according to the flesh, but according to the Spirit.

Psalm 22:22
I will declare Your name to My brethren;
In the midst of the assembly I will praise You.

Which verse, or verses, speaks to your heart the most? Why?

_____

_____

_____

_____

_____

_____

Which verse is on your mind the most?
Pray to God and tell Him what your thoughts are about the verse.

_____

The Way I See It....

by Christopher Foster

Leaving everything behind and running for your life as David had to do would be extremely difficult. I am trying to imagine... leaving, without notice, the people in my life that I love and care for, such as family and friends, and to possibly never see them again...leaving my home, my job... maybe leaving behind plans and dreams.   For me, this is almost impossible to imagine! There's one thing for sure: I cannot imagine going through something like this without God.

David knew God was with him. He also knew he would be going through some tough times.

In Matthew 5:10, the Lord says, "Blessed are those who are persecuted for righteousness' sake, for theirs is the kingdom of God." David was being heavily persecuted during this time, but through his trust in Jesus, he was able to persevere.

If I am truly to live as Christ wants me to live, then I can also expect to be persecuted and to suffer throughout some time in my life here on earth. It may not be as extreme as David's suffering. Then again, it may be, but suffering nonetheless. I know because God's Word says so: in 2 Timothy 3:12, it is declared, "Yes, and all who desire to live godly in Christ Jesus will suffer persecution."

It will always be easier to live the way of the world. That is, do what I want when I want.

However, life is not fully lived unless it is challenging, and one big challenge is living daily for God. I need to remind myself daily of this challenge, and find comfort in knowing that when I live fully for Him, I am receiving the Lord's blessing. No life challenges equal boredom!

Chapter 5

All for Him

We have been made numb by our media. Movies, music, videos, and television makes horror, grief, and sin seem normal; therefore, we are numb to it. Furthermore, media uses all the newest technologies to entertain us. All the toots and whistles are included to keep us mesmerized. Those that work in media know how to keep you watching and listening with wide eyes. They work hard at going almost too far so that you will want to see what happens next.

Surely you have noticed that there are no special sound effects going on as you read of the adventures between David and Saul. There is no background music playing as you read of David's flee and Saul's anger. Perhaps you have also noticed that there are not any exclamation marks to convey intense emotions. Nowhere is it written, "Can you believe it?" or "Then, all of a sudden…" or "…and their lives were to be forever changed…"

However, unlike most of media, the events in the Bible are true. There is no greater toot and whistle than drawing closer to the heart of God. There is nothing media can do to match that. Therefore, God does not have to or need to give His words to you in a fancy and elaborate way, but just as true as they actually are. The result is life changing and guides you to eternity with Him. When we get even just a tiny glimpse of His greatness, we will be compelled to do all for just Him.

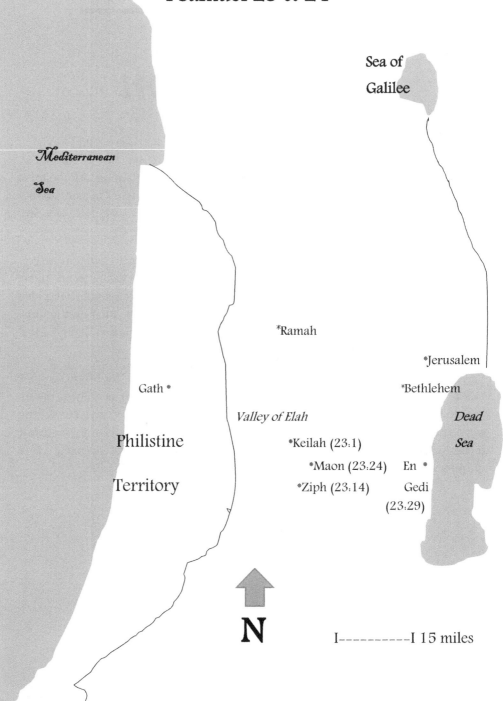

Israel

I Samuel 23 & 24

Sea of
Galilee

Mediterranean

Sea

*Ramah

*Jerusalem

Gath *

*Bethlehem

Dead

Valley of Elah

Philistine

*Keilah (23:1)

Sea

*Maon (23:24)   En *

Territory

*Ziph (23:14)   Gedi

(23:29)

N

I----------I 15 miles

100

Lesson 1

For "Reign" Language

Day 1

Read I Samuel 23: 1-15

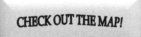

Explanations in your reading:

v. 1   "...robbing the threshing floors."   The threshing floors were the ground of harvested crops.   The Philistines were stealing their food.

v. 6   "... with an ephod..."   Remember, Saul killed all the priests in Nob.   When an ephod was seen, they knew it belonged to Abiathar.   Saul's men believed Abiathar was most likely with David.

v. 10   "...your servant..."   A synonym for "I."   This is in the Bible many times.   Here, David is referring to himself.   He is talking to God, so he is calling himself "God's servant."   (A helpful practice in reading the Bible is to write "I" in your Bible when you see "your servant."   Just read carefully.   There are a few times (very few) it does not mean "I.")

Write a summary of the reading and your own thoughts:

_____

_____

_____

_____

_____

Apply & Obey

David prayed. He prayed to God before making a move. He even asked the Lord more than once the same question to be clear of God's direction.

God answered. We do not actually hear the sound, tone, pitch, and frequency of God's voice when we ask Him for an answer in our lives, not yet. But as servants of God, there are ways of knowing when and how He is speaking to you and what He is saying.

First of all, you have to learn God's language. Someone of a different language is not going to know what you are saying in a conversation, and you will not know what they are saying. However, the more you two get together and communicate, you will start understanding the person more and more.

You speak to God through prayer by sharing with Him all that is in your heart. Then, He will speak to you in so many ways: through others, through an event that happens in your life, through a sermon, through a song, or through His creation. However, *and most importantly*, God will speak to you through your *daily* reading of the Bible.

God promises He will make time for you if you will make time for Him.

LIVE IT!

On the following page, you will see a calendar with 40 days. Take that page out of this book and hang it somewhere clearly visible (on the refrigerator, the bathroom mirror, over your bed or nightstand…). For the next forty days, try to pray at the same time every single day. Of course, you can pray more than once a day, but at least one of those praying times should be at the same time every day. A helpful suggestion is to pray in the morning when you wake up or at night before you go to sleep.

Then, on the calendar, starting with Day 1, write down the time that you prayed. Here's the goal: pray every day at the same time for 40 days. Not every other day, not weekly, but every single day.

If you miss a day, dust yourself off, and pick up where you left off. If you miss two days, start over. Praying at the same time every day for as long as forty days will help create a habit. The purpose of this challenge is so that praying will become part of your daily routine, like brushing your teeth.

The perfect and essential companion to prayer is your Bible. Have your Bible with you when you pray. Soak in its powerful words. This is the strongest way God can speak to you.

At the top of the calendar, copy **Jeremiah 33:3**, and memorize. Then, share the verse with three people, and add the verse to your index cards and/or memory verses list.

Jeremiah 33:3

The Way I See It...

In I Samuel 23, the city of Keilah was being invaded by the Philistines. At the time, David was "on the run" and was in no shape to support or fight for the people of this city.

However, David was an inherently selfless man. He was not concerned about his safety and whether he would be found and killed by Saul. David's thoughts and concerns were consistently projected outward and not inward. In times of trials, whether personal or for the inhabitants of Keilah, he gave it all to God. He did not depend on himself, or search himself for the answers. Instead, he searched God, and looked for the fundamental wisdom that only He can provide. Being courageous enough to give it all to God is a personal struggle that I deal with on a daily basis, especially when times are rough or if God doesn't answer my prayers when I want Him to. I need to be less selfish and more selfless like David. For me to be selfless, and depend solely on God and His timing, I need to be patient and have faith. God's Word says in James 1:2-5, "My brethren, count it all joy when you fall into various trials, knowing that the testing of your faith produces patience. But let patience have its perfect work that you may be perfect and complete, lacking nothing. If any of you lacks wisdom, let him ask of God, who gives to all liberally and without reproach, and it will be given to him."

God's Word clearly states that if I have patience, faith, and seek Him then I will be provided the wisdom to make the right and selfless decisions during times of trials. These verses from James are remarkable words to meditate on as I grow in my walk with Him.

Lesson 2
My Father, the Conductor

Day 1

Read I Samuel 23: 16-29.

Write a summary of the reading and your own thoughts:

_____

_____

_____

_____

_____

Read

Apply

Obey

Pray

The chase is on! This reading is as exciting as any adventure or suspense book you can read; however, this one is true. Is that not awesome!

Unfortunately for David, living a suspenseful life is not all fun. Actually, this time in his life was hard for him. David's heart was probably broken as he had to run from someone that he loved. He was likely hungry, dirty, and fearful of his own life. In his eyes, this time would probably be considered a very sad part of his life.

. . . . . .

Day 2

Read Psalm 54.

Here is David's own words to give you an understanding of how he felt. Underline verses that you like or want to memorize.

Day 3

Saul and David are on the same mountain. Saul's men were making a complete circle around the bottom of the mountain so there would be nowhere for David to go. Then, when it looks like David will be captured, and when it looks like he has no way out, the pursuit suddenly ends.... Interesting, eh?

Apply & Obey

Those Philistines were ungodly, wicked warriors. It is interesting that they attacked a nearby area just as David is almost captured! Is it a coincidence? The answer is "no." As a man of God, take the word "coincidence" out of your vocabulary. It is a pagan word. Nothing in the life of a Christian is by chance nor a coincidence. Everything is orchestrated by God. God's Holy Word clearly says so many times. Carefully read and think about each verse:

> **Colossians 1:17** And He is before all things, and in Him all things consist.

> **Romans 8:28** And we know that all things work together for good to those who love God, to those who are the called according to His purpose.

> **Romans 11:36** For of Him and through Him and to Him are all things, to whom be glory forever. Amen.

These Philistines did not attack out on their own. They may have thought God had nothing to do with it, but God had everything to do with it! God was there. Through the Philistines, God protected David.

God is here. This day is by God. Whether a good day, boring day, or a really bad day, it is by God.

LIVE IT!

Write and memorize **Romans 11:36.**

_____

_____

_____

_____

Share the verse with three people and add to your index cards and/or memory verse list.

Now, list at least 3 things going on in your life right now that you see as bad, could be better, or things you wish were different:

1. _____

_____

2. _____

_____

3. _____

_____

Once your list is made, pray with all your heart to God about each one. Then, under each bad thing, write down how God can give you joy, peace, and comfort for each item you listed. You may just find God leading your answers as He led

David in the Psalms he wrote. Or, you may not know how you can have joy and peace in your circumstance. If you do not feel God has given you an answer to what you have written above, then He wants you to wait for the answer and hold on to Him. In **Psalm 40:1**, David says, "I waited patiently on the LORD; and He inclined to me, and heard my cry." Remember, God has EVERTHING in His hands.

• • • • • •

Day 4

Read **Psalm 57.** Underline or write out any verses that you like.

_____

Pray and thank God for showing you His powerful presence.

_____

The Way I See It...

by Christopher Foster

As young Christian men, we are to be encouraging to others. Encouragement from others has given me peace and happiness when sad. It has given me strength at some weak times, and encouragement has given me confidence when I had none.

When I encourage others, it takes the focus off me, and puts it on the one being encouraged.

For me, therein lies the problem, the weakness. Receiving words of encouragement is, many times, much easier than giving words of encouragement, and my sinful flesh doesn't want the spotlight on anyone else but my own self. This is a personal struggle for me, and I need to remind myself daily the importance of sharing words of encouragement with others, especially those closest to me.

In I Samuel 23: 16-18, Jonathan comes to David in the wilderness, and encourages him that he will be safe and no harm will come to him. These words from his good friend had to have given him confidence and a sense of peace. The same is true for us as Christian men today. We should strive to encourage daily our friends and family.

Lesson 3
Nature Calls

Day 1

Read I Samuel 24 (the whole chapter).

Explanations in your reading:

24:2   "Rocks of the Wild Goats" – this is in En Gedi, which mountainous and rocky with cliffs, which is perfect for goats. Everybody knew that was where the wild goats lived, so their home become a landmark.

24:3 "…attend to his needs…" Saul had personal matters to attend to and excused himself into a nearby cave. Changing his clothes, using the bathroom, combing his hair, caring for a wound – any of these things and more could have been how Saul attended to his needs. It just so happens to be the same cave where David is hiding!

Write a summary and your own thoughts of the reading:

_____

_____

_____

_____

_____

• • • • • •

Day 2

Apply & Obey

David had a chance to kill Saul. The days of living in the woods and living in caves could have been over for David. Kill Saul and go home, or let him live and stay in caves. David chose the cave-life. David's friends encouraged him: "Kill him! Kill him! Here's your chance!" Although very tempting, David kept his focus on his great God: "No, he's God's anointed, and my master." David's actions were out of his love for God. Also, David respected Saul.

LIVE IT!

Write down and memorize **Colossians 3:23.** After memorizing, share this verse with three people, and add to your index cards and/or memory verses list.

_____

_____

_____

_____

We are to respect authority. Yet, have you noticed? . . . it is easier to respect a kind, wise, and fair leader, whose ruling we agree with. Respecting authority that we do not like is not so easy. Nonetheless, David did it.

Authority includes your parents, your grandparents, your pastor at church, your teachers, the principal, your Sunday school teachers, the president, or elders of the church. To respect them means to listen to them and obey, to speak *kindly* and *mannerly*, and to be *grateful* for their guidance in your life.

Whether you like them or not, respect them. Honestly, they do not have to like you either (besides your parents and grandparents). The point of respecting authority is never to be liked. Your Lord Jesus was not liked by a whole bunch of people. We do not respect others to be liked, we respect because God tells us to in His word, and because it gets us closer to God's heart!

Read

Apply

Obey

Pray

In other words, and quite frankly, if you do not respect and honor and obey all of authority that God has placed in your life, you do not honor God, you do not respect God, and you are not obeying Him.

LIVE IT!

When you respect authority, you are obeying God. Write down a list of people of authority that are in your life:

_____

_____

_____

_____

_____

_____

_____

God has given these people very important roles – one role being to guide and care for you. It is a tough job. They need the power of prayer. Your prayers help them guide you correctly and in God's will.

Before closing this Bible study, pray for the leaders in your life.
Ask for specific blessings for each.
For example, pray Mom gets a good night's rest,
pray for your pastor's health and family,
pray that the president turns his life to Jesus....

The Way I See It...

by Christopher Foster

There are several of the Ten Commandments that are not illegal in the eyes of current laws; however, all are important commandments for a growing man of God.

If I had to pick one commandment of greatest importance for a growing young man, I would pick commandment number five. God says in Exodus 20:12, "Honor your father and your mother, that your days may be long upon the land which the Lord your God is giving you."

I was pretty good at doing this growing up, because my parents instilled in me the importance of honoring not only them, but God at a young age. It is not to say that I didn't have days where I could have done a better job, and on those days I was quickly reminded of my blunder.

Learning to honor is just that; it is learning. I made several mistakes as I was learning to honor my parents, but mistakes are part of the learning process. I learned from my mistakes, and was able to apply what I had learned as I grew into a young man and then into an adult.

Not only did learning to honor my parents at a young age support my understanding of how to honor God, it also supported my understanding of how to honor other figures in position of authority. Likewise, this helps me honor God.

Lesson 4
Let Us Reflect

The last three lessons have been packed full of exposures. Exposures? Good question, yes, exposing truth of your life and how God sees it. The lessons may have brought a bit of discomfort to you, or maybe a refreshed or new understanding of things in your life that are holding you back from walking with God. They are so important in helping you grow into a Godly man. It is time to review and get some encouragement!

Lesson 1: David prayed to God for guidance, and God answered. God always answers. Remember your prayer challenge? Are you praying at the same time every day? Sometimes it is hard to know what to say when we pray, and the same words of prayer come out over and over. Then, it sometimes feels like no connection with God has been made, but we keep praying, because "it's the right thing to do." Hopefully the following prayer guide will help:

- Did you talk to your Mom or Dad today? Ask God the same questions, or make the same comments to God.
- Are you sad or upset? Share it with God completely. Are you mad? Talk it over with God. Are you happy? Give thanks to God. Are you feeling normal and ordinary? Think of others who need your prayer.
- What has been on your mind today? Your ball game? Music lesson? Spelling test? Family vacation? Whatever it is, talk about it to God.
- Are you feeling guilty about a sin in your life? Talk to God about it. Tell Him you are sorry. Ask God for forgiveness. Then, forget about it. God did.
- Tell the truth: "God, I don't know what to say." You may find that just spending time quietly with no words with God floods you with His strong presence, His joy, and His love.

 Keep Praying!

Lesson 2: David seemed trapped and destined to be killed by Saul and his men. Although, things *seemed* that way, God had another plan.

God is the conductor, and the entire world is His orchestra. You are in that orchestra. The piece of music you are playing is the Bible. Do not worry if you mess up. God is the conductor, not you. He will fix it. Also, do not worry if you do not know how to play certain parts of the "music." He will show you how. Do the big "tubas" in the world make you fearful? No worries, God has them under His control. Just keep making music!

Lesson 3: When you respect authority, you are loving God. David respected Saul because David loved God. Do you get tired of being told what to do and what not to do? Thank God for that. It is just another opportunity that God has given you to show Him that you love Him.

LIVE IT!

Re-memorize your last three memory verses, share each verse with three people. They are written out here in the New King James version.

Jeremiah 33:3 "Call to Me, and I will answer you, and show you great and mighty things, which you do not know.

Romans 11:36 For of Him and through Him and to Him are all things, to whom be glory forever. Amen.

Colossians 3:23   *And whatever you do, do it heartily, as to the Lord and not to men.*

Choose one of the last three lessons to talk about with a parent or another Godly man in your life.

Which lesson do you choose?

_____

Write down further thoughts and questions you have about the lesson, or what you would like to discuss with a Godly leader in your life.

_____

_____

_____

_____

_____

_____

Pray and talk to God about your closer walk with Him.

_____

In this chapter, David had to learn to live in the world, but for God. He wrote a great Psalm that undoubtedly helped him through it.

Read Psalm 1.

Underline verses you like or that you would like to memorize. The verses in Psalm one are among the most essential verses for a man to hide in his heart.

If you would like write down any thoughts you have of reading Psalm 1.

_____

_____

_____

_____

_____

_____

_____

_____

_____

Pray asking God to help you reflect Him as you are engaged with others.

Chapter 6

The Valley of the Shadow of Death

Hopefully, you are enjoying the book of I Samuel. It has everything: suspense, chases, adventure, joy, despair, even a little blood and guts. . . and that's not even the best part. You are there, too. Within the very thick of their lives, the lives of David and Saul, within all the hunger, despair, and uncertainty, you were in the heart and mind of God through it all. God knew you would be reading about their lives. He knew there would be a time, through learning about David, in which you would want to know more.

Can you imagine living a life of constant hiding? It is hard to even imagine. It could be compared to hide-and-go-seek, except if you are caught, you are not "it," you are captured and possibly killed.

David's first thought when he woke up was, "I am still alive." He would live through the day, constantly mindful that he may be captured or killed at any time.

Pray before each study, and ask God to speak to you through His Word. Share a hunger with David – a hunger to grow closer to God.

Israel

1 Samuel 25, 26, & 27

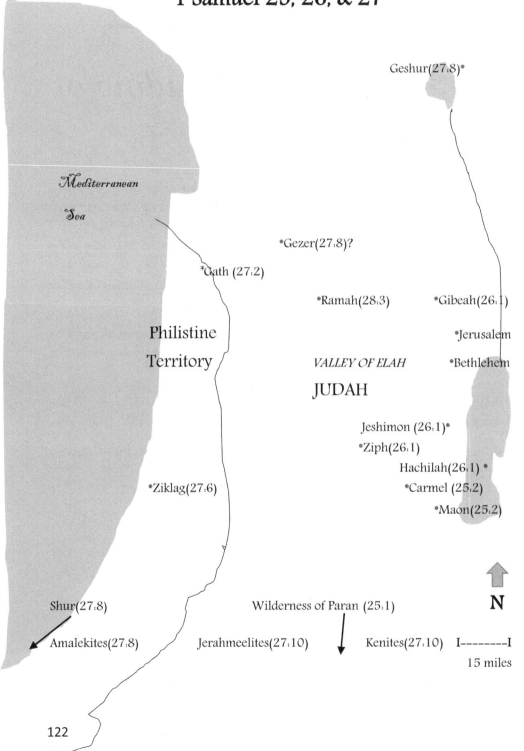

Geshur(27:8)*

Mediterranean

Sea

*Gezer(27:8)?

*Gath (27:2)

*Ramah(28:3)   *Gibeah(26:1)

Philistine   *Jerusalem

Territory   *Bethlehem

VALLEY OF ELAH

JUDAH

Jeshimon (26:1)*

*Ziph(26:1)

Hachilah(26:1) *

*Ziklag(27:6)   *Carmel (25:2)

*Maon(25:2)

N

Shur(27:8)   Wilderness of Paran (25:1)

Amalekites(27:8)   Jerahmeelites(27:10)   Kenites(27:10)   I--------I
                                                                          15 miles

Lesson 1
Help! Help!

Day 1

CHECK OUT THE MAP!

Read I Samuel 25: 1-12.

Explanations of your reading:

v. 3   "... the house of Caleb." More about Caleb can be learned in the book of Joshua. He was no longer alive in the book of Samuel. Caleb was a great warrior for God. Hebron in Judah belonged to Caleb.

v. 7   "... nor was there anything missing..." They did not go without what they needed. David and his men helped them.

v. 8   "... to your servants..." Remember, this translates as "to us." They are calling themselves Nabal's servants as a sign of respect, similar to the way we say "Yes sir/no sir" to show respect.

Write a summary of the reading and your own thoughts:

_____

_____

_____

_____

_____

• • • • • •

Day 2

Apply & Obey

Answer the following questions to help you with understanding:

Was Nabal a giving and generous man? _____

Who cared for Nabal's shearers as they worked in Carmel, Nabal or David?
_____

Do you think Nabal was aware of his workers' safety and well-being as they worked in the field of Carmel?
_____

Does   Nabal   show   care   or   concern   for   his   shearers?
_____

What was Nabal's reason for not helping David?
_____
_____

LIVE IT!

Look up **Luke 10:2.** Write the verse here and memorize.

_____
_____
_____
_____

Share the verse with three people and add to your index cards and/or memory verses list.

Consider your answers to these questions:

Do you know the names of everyone in the world? _____

Do you know the names of everyone in your country? _____

Your state? _____

How about in your city? _____

Do you know the names of all the people that go to your school or to your church? _____

Please listen carefully: we are not to help only others that we know. We do not have to know why someone needs help. Someone who needs your help may not be pretty or nice. They may not be rich or fun. Those who need your help may be unattractive, smelly, and poor. This is who Jesus helped.

Start helping others more. Are you wondering how? Ask God. He will show you, possibly when you are least expecting it and when you would rather not. However, you will grow closer to Him in your obedience.

One good starting point is with your parents. Help whether you want to or not. Make a daily habit of saying, "How can I help you?"

Read

Apply

Obey

Pray

Help others at church or school. At church, help other boys or girls find their classes. Help find a Bible verse. Help clean a mess. Help by holding a door open for others. As school, help a classmate with school work. Help someone carry a heavy load. Help someone smile.

By helping others, you open up new friendships. When you open new friendships, you show you care. When you show you care, you have paved a way to share salvation through Jesus with others.

LIVE IT!

There are many servants of God that pray every morning at 10:02. Why 10:02? It is based on your memory verse, and Jesus's words in **Luke 10:2:**

Then He said to them, "The harvest truly is great, but the laborers are few; therefore pray the Lord of the harvest to send out laborers into His harvest."

Jesus sees that there are so many people that need love, hope, and salvation. They need help. Yet, there are so few that are actually willing to help. We need to be His laborers, and we need to pray for one another. Would you like to join your fellow servants in prayer at 10:02 am?

Think of where you usually are and what you are usually doing at 10:02am. Not to take time away from study time at school, but a quick yet heartfelt prayer can be powerful. Remember to pray at this time: "God, help me, Your laborer, to be a helper and witness for Jesus to the lost and hopeless, Your harvest."

• • • • • •

Day 3

Read **Matthew 25:35-40.** Copy and memorize **Matthew 25:40** (not the whole passage, just verse 40):

_____

_____

_____

_____

_____

Young men and young ladies all around you need help. They *need* your help. Like Nabal, do not come up with an excuse why you cannot help someone. Be a laborer for Christ today and every day.

> EVEN ADULTS, LIKE MOM & DAD, MUST SOMETIMES BE CAUTIOUS WHEN LENDING A HAND TO STRANGERS. IF YOU KNOW OF AN ADULT IN NEED, INFORM YOUR PARENTS AND/OR TEACHERS. IT'S A SAFE RULE OF THUMB.

_____

Pray for the Holy Spirit to give you the ability to see with His eyes, so that you can see how much God loves those who seem like "the least of these."

_____

Lesson 2
Chill!

Read I Samuel 25:13-44.

Write a summary and your own thoughts of the reading:

_____

_____

_____

_____

_____

Although many men during this time period had more than one wife, it was not with God's blessing. This was part of their culture that overshadowed God's perfect structure of marriage. If you think about it, our society today overshadows much of God's law.

· · · · · ·

Day 2

Apply & Obey

Read verse 13 again. Would you agree David is very angry? Remember, David has been hiding in the woods, living in caves, hoping every minute of every day he is not found and killed. Many days without sleep, food, and water. David mourns for Samuel while hiding, dirty and hungry.

Read Psalm 38, and you will know, in David's own words, how he felt. There may be a verse or two in the chapter that reflects how   you have felt before. Write down words David used to describe how he felt:

_____

_____

_____

_____

_____

• • • • • •
Day 3

Now that you have a better understanding of what David was going through, let's proceed. David and his friends know there is a wealthy man in town that could be of great help. But this man Nabal says, "Forget it. Get lost. Not my problem."

Ouch!

That was the tiny one ounce of patience that David had left. This was "the straw that broke the camel's back." David planned to not just get even; David planned to kill. David is sick, sore, achy and hungry, and then snubbed by a rich man!

Nabal deserves to have his head pinched right off, doesn't he? He is the bad guy in this adventure-packed Book. But here's the thing: if David had attacked Nabal, David would have been acting on his anger and all about what *he* wanted, and not necessarily *God's will*. By acting on his emotions, David would have made a big mistake. **We will make wrong choices when we act on our emotions.** If not for Abigail, who stopped David from acting on his anger, everything could have gotten even worse for David.

As a Christian, although you have been given much, you will have hard times and you will be persecuted. As you try to do all you can to become a godly man, bad things are going to happen. You will make mistakes. People are going to discourage you, laugh at you, and mistreat you. Then, emotions happen. Anger happens.

LIVE IT!

Write and memorize **Psalm 55:22:**

_____

_____

_____

_____

_____

Once memorized, share the verse with three people and add to your index cards and/or memory verses list.

God will give you patience to control your anger. God will give you self-control so that you do not act foolishly when you are angry.

Can you think of any other emotions that need to be controlled in your own life, such as anger, sadness, self-pity, defeat, jealousy, hate, greediness, or bitterness? Write out some emotions that you have felt lately that you think you need to control:

Read

Apply

Obey

Pray

_____

_____

_____

Now is a good time to pray to God and submit to His guidance. How can the emotions you listed be controlled? (See if any of these words help you: love, joy, peace, patience, kindness, goodness, faithfulness, gentleness, self-control.)

_____

_____

_____

_____

Read David's God-inspired words in Psalm 139:23, 24.
Pray these words to God.

The Way I See It...

by Christopher Foster

The Bible tells me how to be a husband. Ephesians 5:25 says, "Husbands, love your wives, just as Christ also loved the church and gave Himself for her." That's pretty astounding for me to think about! My love should equal to that of Christ's love for the church. Jesus loves His church. He provides and cares for His church. He longs to be with His church forever, and He gave His life for his church. This is how I am to love my wife.

This is possible for me only when the Word is kept close to my heart, with the love of God within me.

Furthermore, God is preparing a lady especially for you, and you can pray for her now.

Having guidance for life from the Bible is the only right way to live. Ephesians 5:25 shows me of the importance of holding my wife in high regard. Consequently, I see her as far greater and more beautiful than precious rubies!

Lesson 3
Sleep With One Eye Open!

Day 1

Read I Samuel 26.

CHECK OUT THE MAP!

Explanations in your reading:

v. 1   The Ziphites can be fun to discuss! . . . tattle-tales? . . . loyal to their king? . . .

v. 2   Why 3,000 men to seek one man? David has approximately 400 men with him. If Saul thought he needed to have 3,000 men, he must really tremble at just the thought of David. Of course, remember, Saul *did* actually witness David killing a giant, *and* David killed 200 Philistines. Consequently, Saul is probably somewhat smart for fearing David, but 3,000 men???

Write a summary and your own thoughts of the reading:

_____

_____

_____

_____

_____

· · · · · ·

Day 2

Great chapter! David is given yet another opportunity to kill Saul, and again, chooses not to go through with it. Saul takes 3,000 men to find David, and they all go to bed and sleep.

Can you imagine? . . .

. . . It is dark. All the men (3000), taking up a great deal of space, perhaps similar to an entire campground, find a comfortable place to camp and sleep for the night. All is quiet...

Then, coming out of the dark woods, are two men (David and Abishai) tiptoeing slowly into the camp. Sneaking slap-in-the- middle of 3,000 sleeping men! Stepping over this one, accidentally kicking that one, they search for the king. Quite a daring adventure!

Apply & Obey

The words of David in verse 24 prove that he was positively a man after God's own heart:

". . . let my life be valued much in the eyes of the LORD, and let Him deliver me out of all tribulation."

David was talking to Saul, and explaining the reason why he did not kill Saul. In other words, "What would God think of me if I did that?"

LIVE IT!

Write down **1 Samuel 26:24**, and memorize:

_____

_____

_____

_____

_____

Once you have the verse memorized, share the verse with three people, and add to your index cards and/or memory verses list.

As a brother in Christ, God is your real Dad. The father you have here on earth is also your Dad. He was appointed by God to love and care for you, and to be a *reflection* of your real Father. Therefore, completely loving your earthly father with all your heart and being grateful for him is so important in your growth with God.

Also, whether you realize it or not, you feel great when your earthly father is proud of you. Make your heavenly Father proud as well!

Now, always remember that God is not going to love you more if you make Him proud. He already loves you completely. He died in *your* place to die so that He can be with you forever. He loved you first.

There is really only one thing that I want out of this earthly life, and that is to one day hear God, my Dad, say the same words to me that He said to Jesus:

Matthew 3:17b

"This is My beloved Son [child], in whom I am well pleased."

No riches on earth can bring more joy. Nothing else comes close.

How can we, like David, make our choices in life to please God? Here are the 3 biggest ways:

1. Surrender your life to Jesus Christ. Give it all to Him, and trust Him with it.
2. Read your Bible every day.
3. Pray to God and share your heart with Him all throughout the day, every day.

Through these simple steps that you have heard since you were a little boy, the Holy Spirit will transcend your life. You will *want* to live completely for God.

Pray for God's guidance in walking with Him daily.

Lesson 4

All Have Gone Astray...

Day 1

Read I Samuel 27.

CHECK OUT THE MAP!

Write a summary of the reading and your own thoughts:

_____

_____

_____

_____

_____

No, this is not good. Are you confused? Are you thinking, "Did I read this right?" or "This can't be right!" or just a good, "Huh?"

If any of this chapter seems a bit confusing, then you are absolutely right! In Chapter 27, we see a man without God. This is another reason we should love the Bible. It is not all butterflies and daisies. It is the truth; it is real. God shows us where David sunk low, and He shows us what happens as a result.

David says at the beginning of the chapter, "Saul's going to kill me!" It sounds as if David has decided what will happen to him instead of allowing God to decide. Also, did we not just read where David and Saul make peace? Granted, Saul should not be trusted; nevertheless, we all of a sudden see that David is still in hiding and fearing like never before for his life. David did not seek God.

David and 600 men and their families move to live with and fight with the Philistines. Also, they will serve the king in the Philistines.

• • • • • •

Day 2

Apply & Obey

Sweet brother in Christ, please take a moment to understand that the fears, the temptations, and the defeats that you will face just may stomp your heart and leave you feeling alone. Understand that you are not alone.

How many times in the Bible does God instruct us not to fear? (If you are not sure, go investigate, and then come back.) _____

LIVE IT!

Here are two verses for you to hide in your heart:

1. Write and memorize **Deuteronomy 20:4:**

_____

_____

_____

_____

2. Write and memorize **Galations 6:9:**

_____

_____

_____

_____

Once memorized, share both verses with three people and write them on your index cards and/or add them to your memory verses lists.

Are you still praying every day at the same time? If not, do not fear. Just start again.

• • • • • •

Day 3

LIVE IT!

Take one of your index cards, and write these words:

"Where are you?"

These words were spoken by God to Adam and Eve after they sinned and were *afraid* for God to see them (Genesis 3:9). God knew where they were, but their hearts were no longer close to God's heart. God wanted them back. So God cried out, "Where are you?"

Is God crying that out to you? Place this index card by your bedside so you can see God's words as soon as you wake up. Then answer Him. That is, pray to God about whatever is in your heart and on your mind. Let God know "where" you are.

Pray and ask our mighty God to help you to always remember to turn to Him.

Lesson 5

Stop and Think About It...

You have learned so much of the Bible, of David, and hopefully, of God and of yourself. What are your thoughts so far in this spiritual journey? How do you feel God has spoken to you? Or, what part of this Bible study seems to be a heavy thought in your mind?

_____

_____

_____

_____

Why is it important to memorize verses?

_____

_____

_____

_____

Re-memorize the following verses:

Luke 10:2
Then He said to them, "The harvest truly *is* great, but the laborers *are* few; therefore pray the Lord of the harvest to send out laborers into His harvest."

Matthew 25:40
And the King will answer and say to them, 'Assuredly, I say to you, inasmuch as you did *it* to one of the least of these My brethren, you did *it* to Me.'

Psalm 55:22
Cast your burden on the LORD,
And He shall sustain you;
He shall never permit the righteous to be moved.

1 Samuel 26:24
"And indeed, as your life was valued much this day in my eyes, so let my life be valued much in the eyes of the LORD, and let Him deliver me out of all tribulation."

Deuteronomy 20:4
For the LORD your God *is* He who goes with you, to fight for you against your enemies, to save you.

Galatians 6:9
And let us not grow weary while doing good, for in due season we shall reap if we do not lose heart.

Once you feel you know them well, share all six verses with three people. Then, let each person know which verse you like the best.

Pray that you keep God's words in your heart as you grow.

Chapter 7

Stand Strong

The next four lessons will wrap up the First Book of Samuel. Hopefully, you agree that it is an awesome book in the Bible. Much has happened since we first started the study, from David's boyhood to entering manhood living in the woods, to moving to Philistine territory.

What about you? What has happened in your life? Not to focus necessarily on bad things, and not to focus necessarily on just good things; yet, how has God made happenings in your life? What has He shown you about Himself? What has He shown you about yourself? What do you still want to know?

Where have you grown spiritually? Where in your life have you realized you may have a weakness to sin? Jesus is holding out his hands and saying, "I'll take it away." Believe, and let Him.

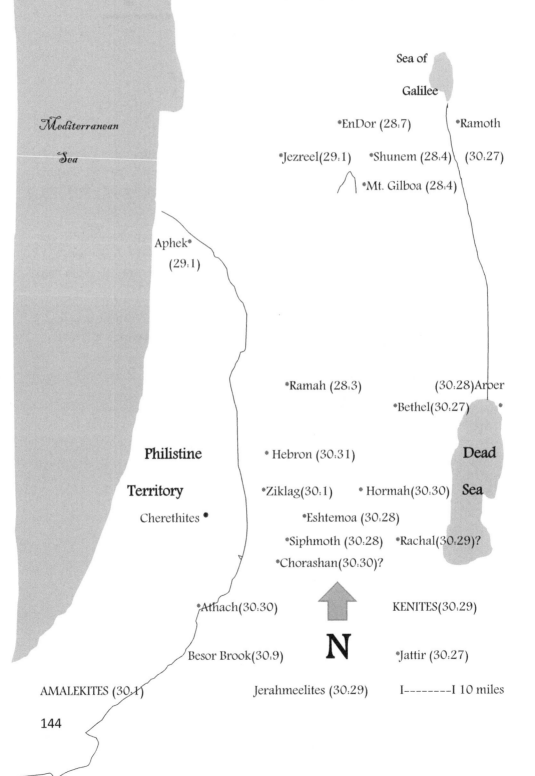

Israel

1 Samuel 28, 29, & 30

Mediterranean

Sea

Sea of

Galilee

*EnDor (28:7)   *Ramoth

*Jezreel(29:1)   *Shunem (28:4)   (30:27)

*Mt. Gilboa (28:4)

Aphek*

(29:1)

*Ramah (28:3)   (30:28)Arœr

*Bethel(30:27)

Philistine   * Hebron (30:31)   **Dead**

Territory   *Ziklag(30:1)   * Hormah(30:30)   **Sea**

Cherethites *   *Eshtemoa (30:28)

*Siphmoth (30:28)   *Rachal(30:29)?

*Chorashan(30:30)?

N

*Athach(30:30)   KENITES(30:29)

Besor Brook(30:9)   *Jattir (30:27)

AMALEKITES (30:1)   Jerahmeelites (30:29)   I--------I 10 miles

144

Lesson 1

Be Careful Little Eyes and Ears!

Day 1

Read I Samuel 28.

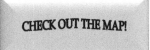

Explanations in your reading:

v. 2   ". . . your servant "

Remember, this is a synonym for "I."

v. 3   ". . . the mediums and spiritists. . ." These are fortune tellers and those who try to contact the dead without the authority of God.

v. 4   You will find Shunem and Gilboa in the northern part of Israel.

v. 6   ". . . Urim. . ." Urim is a piece on a prophet's ephod, which represents finding God's way clearly. It is a Hebrew word meaning "light." Saul may have been trying to find God's direction, or a "lighted way" to see more clearly through some prophet.

v. 8   ". . . a séance." A séance is a practice of witchcraft to bring the dead back and speak with them. Considering this is done without the authority of God, the Devil can make his own presence very powerful.

v. 9   The woman, at this time, does not know that the disguised man is Saul.

v. 10   "As the LORD lives. . ." Many, like Saul, proclaim God's name, yet will not give God their lives.

v. 14   ". . . a mantle. . ." A robe.

v. 15   "Why have you disturbed me by bringing me up?" Our physical, earthly bodies are buried. If Samuel appeared in a physical form, his physical earthly body was brought up from the grave.

Write a summary and your own thoughts of the reading: ( )

_____

_____

_____

_____

SPOOKY!!!

Contacting demonic spirits is a dangerous sin. Saul's decision to visit this witch just illustrates that he is a godless man. Saul learns nothing. He sits with the witch and stuffs his belly. No repentance for sins. No praise to God.

> ... *trouble will come to him who seeks evil.*
> *Proverbs 11:27*

Although this a dark and evil place to be, God reigns. God turned this ugliness around. In verse 18, the consequences of disobedience are made known. God's will is made known. God's truth is made known.

• • • • • •

Day 2

Apply & Obey

There are so many mystery and adventure books available to read today. Many are mystical, magical, haunting, suspenseful, and thrilling. These books are also fiction, aren't they? Chapter 28 in 1 Samuel is the truth. Demons are real. Witchcraft is real. God says it is evil. One reason it is evil is because it is seeking out a spirit other than the Holy Spirit. It is saying, "Go away God, you are not good enough. I'll find help elsewhere." This is an open door for Satan.

The main characters in the fictional books usually survive, are wiser, and heroic at the end (That is definitely fiction!). In real life, these characters would be without God, without hope, depressed, and angry. Like Saul, they refuse to praise God.

When you are reading a fictional book or watching a movie with witchcraft, it is fiction. Fiction is not always bad, or sinful. Nonetheless, remember, just because it is fiction does not mean it is always OK or good to read. So, what is OK and what is not OK?

If your parents say, "No, do not read it," then you cannot read it. Case closed. If you are reading a book or watching a movie and *you* feel it may be dishonoring the truth and sovereignty of God, then stop. Stop even if you were given permission. This feeling is most likely the Holy Spirit telling you to stop reading this book, or stop watching this movie. This is called **discernment** – knowing when something is pleasing or displeasing to God.

An important point: just because there is sin in a movie or book does not confirm it as bad to watch or read. Every movie or book contains sin. Usually, the whole story is about characters overcoming sin. Also, a fantasy movie or book containing anything from trolls to superheroes can be a fun and entertaining movie or book. However, when the sin is glorified or looked at as "cool," or needed, close the book. Turn off the movie or TV show.

> *Read*
>
> *Apply*
>
> *Obey*
>
> *Pray*

Fantasies come from our imaginations. With your imagination, you are more creative. A sorcerer who loves? Sounds imaginative and creative, and of course, fictional. God wants you to be more creative. It takes creativity to find new inventions.

The bottom line is this: God forbids witchcraft and sorcery. It only strengthens the work of the devil. God promises in Revelation 22:15 that sorcerers will be left outside Heaven's gate with others who "love and practice a lie."

LIVE IT!

Read Deuteronomy 18:9-13. Write a summary of the reading. (An abomination is something deeply hated by God.)

_____

_____

_____

_____

_____

If there are any movies, television shows, or books that you are just not sure about, first of all, ask God. Then wait patiently for and look for His answer. He will answer you. Also, talk to your parents and church leaders.

• • • • • •

Day 3

LIVE IT!

Write and memorize **Proverbs 11:27:**

_____

_____

_____

_____

_____

Share the verse with three people and add the verse to your index cards and/or memory verses list.

_____

Ask God for discernment in your daily walk with Him.

_____

Lesson 2

Lean on Me!

Day 1

Read I Samuel 29.

As you read 1 Samuel 29, keep the map handy. Follow along with where everyone is going. There is a whole lot going on at one time.

Write a summary and your own thoughts of the reading:

_____

_____

_____

_____

_____

• • • • • •

Day 2

You may have noticed that the Philistines controlled the western, coastal side of Israel. They were always wanting more. In trying to get more, they would usually go east into King Saul's territory.

In chapter 29, David is still loyal to the Philistines and ready to fight against his own people, which he is now calling his enemies. King Achish and all the Philistines seem to have more intelligence than David. For the first and only time in the Bible, you may find yourself in agreement with the Philistines!

If you were a Philistine (just imagine), you knew David. You knew he was the one who killed the people of our village a few years ago. Now, he thinks he is going to stand by *you* in battle? The one who is also best friends with King Saul's son? Oh no! No, thanks. Trusting David on the battlefield as a Philistine was just asking too much.

Apply & Obey

David, now rejected by everyone, goes back to live in Philistine territory. What a sad, lonely life! David turned his back on Israel. Now, the Philistines turn their back on David. Although David has men with him, they are simply followers. He is coming close to losing them as well.

Friends are a precious gift from God. Are they perfect? No, but neither are you. Do not grow away from friends. Grow with them! They never get too small. Friends help you grow with Jesus. You help friends grow with Jesus.

It is always great to make new friends; however, never turn your back on a friend, thinking you will have more fun with a different friend. Be loyal to your friends. Pray for them. Add your friend to your prayer list and pray for that friend regularly. God loves friendships.

LIVE IT!

Choose a verse that reminds you of a friendship that you have and copy the verse:

Proverb 17:17   A friend loves at all times.

Proverb 27:10	Do not forsake your own friend or you father's friend.
Psalm 119:63 keep	I am a companion of all who fear You, and of those who Your precepts.
1 John 1:7	But if we walk in the light as He is in the light we have fellowship with one another, and the blood of Jesus Christ His Son cleanses us from all sin.
1 John 2:10	He who loves his brother abides in the light, and there is no cause for stumbling in him.
Ecclesiastes 4:9-10	Two are better than one, because they have a good reward for their labor. For if they fall, one will lift up his companion.
Hebrews 13:1	Let brotherly love continue.

_____

_____

_____

_____

_____

Memorize the verse, and then share the verse with three people, including a good friend. Add the verse to your index cards and/or memory verses list.

Lost friendships are sad; however, any friend that causes you to be further from God, or that encourages you to partake in sin may not be a true friend.

Pray and thank God for the blessing of your friends.
Pray for your friend to grow closer to Jesus
and that God bless him according to His will.

Lesson 3
Homeward Bound

Day 1

Read I Samuel 30.

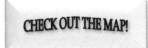
CHECK OUT THE MAP!

Explanations in your reading:

v. 16   "Spoil" is possessions; things taken from another.

v. 15   The Cherethites were possibly part of the Philistine family.

Write a summary and your own thoughts of the reading:

_____

_____

_____

_____

_____

•   •   •   •   •   •

Day 2

David had gone through so many struggles. This guy had it rough! He had left his home in Israel. He lived with the Philistines. He killed many people. Then, he was rejected by the Philistines.

As he was travelling on foot for three days, after the Philistines told him to go away, David was probably thinking, "Where do I go now? What do I do?" In his loneliness, depression, and confusion, things got worse in Ziklag. Now he has no one by his side. Then, he *finally* remembers,

"God?...."

Apply & Obey

David strengthened himself in the Lord his God! God did not forget David. David forgot God. When David finally reached for God, God was right there. God loved David. God gave him strength. God gave him wisdom. God gave him guidance. God gave him love. What a relief to see our good ol' David back!

Now, please do not think you can make wrong choices and sin and do as you please, and then run back into God's arms. Watch it! It did not work for Saul, and David did not come out unbruised!

There are two bad consequences for sin: you grow further away from God (which means you get dumb), and you will be punished.

However, when we do fall short of God's glory (**we have, we do, and we will**), or when tragedy occurs in our lives (**it does, and it will**), *find your strength in the Lord!*

Person after person praised God after thinking they were weak and alone, and yet God Almighty, gave them love and strength. He is our *Jehovah-jireh!*

LIVE IT!

Try to put yourself in the shoes of each one of these persons from the Bible:

- **Job** lost all his children, his health, and all that he owned. In Job 1:21, he proclaims,

"The LORD gave, and the LORD has taken away;

Blessed be the name of the LORD."

- *Nebuchadnezzar* was forced out of his rich and powerful kingdom in Babylon and left in the fields to eat grass and live like an animal. His kingdom was restored before he died. In Daniel 4:37, he proclaims,

> **"Now I, Nebuchadnezzar, praise and extol and**
> **honor the King of heaven, all of whose works are truth,**
> **and His ways justice,…"**

- *Jonah* ran from God and was swallowed by a whale. Jonah proclaims in Jonah 2:2,

> **"I cried out to the LORD because of my affliction, and He answered me."**

and in Jonah 2:6,

> **"Yet You have brought up my life from the pit, O LORD, my God."**

- *Habakkuk* feared the fall of his hometown in Judah. It was about to be overthrown and conquered. Yet he proclaims in Habakkuk 3:18,

> **"Yet I will rejoice in the LORD, I will joy in the God of my salvation."**

- *John,* after being severely brutalized and banished to an island, proclaims in Revelation 1:6,

> **"To Him be the glory and dominion forever and ever. Amen."**

- *Jesus Christ* proclaims in Luke 23:46, just before dying on the cross,

> **"Father, into Your hands I commit My spirit."**

- *David,* running for his life from Saul, proclaims in Psalm 18:1-2,

> **"I will love You, O LORD, my strength. The LORD is my rock and my fortress and my deliverer; My God, my strength, in whom I will trust; My shield and the horn of my salvation, my stronghold. I will call upon the LORD, who is worthy to be praised; so shall I be saved from my enemies."**

And in Psalm 54:6,

"I will freely sacrifice to You, I will praise Your name, O LORD, for it is good."

Day 3

In your own times of trouble, God wants you to see that you can have peace and joy.

He has given you Job, Nebuchadnezzar, Jonah, Habakkuk, John, Jesus, and David for you to read about and know and remember that God is with you. He has given you this insight through the Bible.

Now listen, you will never remember this if you do not read your Bible. You should try your best to read your Bible every day. It is good to surround yourself with the words of God's heart.

Precious brother in Christ, are the words of God easily accessible to you? Get ready to live it....

LIVE IT!

The following is a Word-of-God-Accessibility Checklist. Check EACH ONE once it is *completely* accomplished:

_____ I have at least one Bible that I enjoy reading. (If your Bible is as small as your hand, or if you need a microscope to read the words, then that is not classified as enjoyable reading.)

_____ I know how to access Bible passages and Biblical truths and devotions using the internet.

_____ I have accessed Bible passages and Biblical truths through the internet (perhaps with Mom and Dad's help/supervision). The three sites I have explored include

_____,

_____,

_____.

_____ I can recite at least 3 verses from memory right now.

_____ I have a favorite memory verse. It is

_____

_____

_____

_____

_____ I have at least one memory verse hanging on my wall in my room.

_____ I still have my "Where are you?" index card next to my bed.

_____ I placed a Bible verse in my bathroom so I can see it every day.

_____ I placed a Bible verse in the kitchen so I can read it every day.

_____ I am keeping track of my memory verses from this study, and I try to memorize the verses often. I will continue to do so.

_____ I am reading my Bible every day and I commit to continue doing so.

_____ I can recite the Old and New Testament books.

Big project, eh? Completing this checklist will help pave the way to draw you closer to God, and will give you wisdom. This Word-of-God Accessibility checklist contains tools that you need in your life as you grow.

Pray, and thank God for His big love letter (the Bible) to you so that you can know Him more.

The Way I See It...

by Christopher Foster

In I Samuel 30:21-25, David's men had a hard time understanding why those that did not go into battle should take part in the reward of winning the battle. However, David understood that all of his men played an important role, and that the Lord blessing his men was the reason that the battle was won. It can be very difficult for men to understand that everything that they have is God's, and that their possessions are only theirs because God allows it. This goes back to the instinctually selfish, greedy nature of man. It is very easy for me to think that I have what I have because I earned it, I worked hard for it, and I deserve it. But, this is totally wrong. It is important for me to realize, and remind myself daily that I have what I have because God gave it to me, and it can be taken away. We should thank the Lord daily for our blessings, and give back through our tithes, offerings, gifts, donations, time, and servitude to others.

Chapter 8

A Growing Man

I remember these words from my pastor many years ago: "A man's character is measured by what it takes to stop him." When everything is going wrong, it's your biggest chance to grow.

Seeing my own son suffer, go through pain, or have a bad day is heart-wrenching for me. However, I know that his Godly character will never grow unless he goes through bad times with the rod and staff of his Heavenly Father.

There are grown men who have a character that can presently be measured in inches. They hit hard times and turn to drugs, alcohol, aggression, depression, bitterness, hatefulness, laziness, or they just give up.

Suffering, struggles, and pain are *inevitable* in this life. **Thank God for them!** He is giving you a chance to submit to His Holy Spirit, and to face the challenge, and dare it to come closer. He is giving you a chance to throw away your fear and run to Him. He is giving you a chance to persevere, to be bolder, to be stronger, and to know that He is more powerful than your problem. He is giving you a chance to be wiser. He is giving you a chance to raise your hands to Him and say, "I surrender all to You, God!" He is giving you a chance to see the fruit of obedience to Him.

With God, nothing will stop you, and your character will be immeasurable.

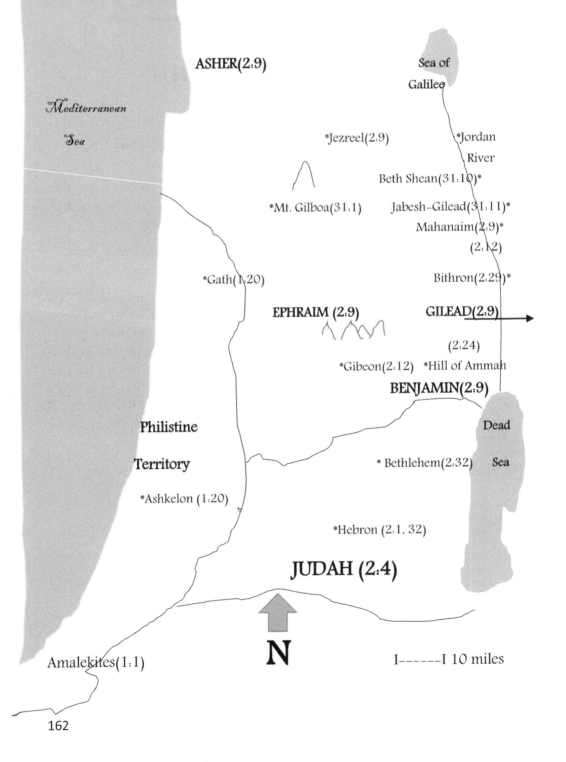

Israel

I Samuel 31 & II Samuel 1, 2

ASHER(2:9)

Sea of
Galilee

Mediterranean

Sea

*Jezreel(2:9)

*Jordan
River

Beth Shean(31:10)*

*Mt. Gilboa(31:1)

Jabesh-Gilead(31:11)*

Mahanaim(2:9)*

(2:12)

Bithron(2:29)*

*Gath(1:20)

EPHRAIM (2:9)

GILEAD(2:9)

(2:24)

*Gibeon(2:12)   *Hill of Ammah

BENJAMIN(2:9)

Dead

Philistine

Sea

Territory

* Bethlehem(2:32)

*Ashkelon (1:20)

*Hebron (2:1, 32)

JUDAH (2:4)

N

Amalekites(1:1)

I------I 10 miles

Lesson 1
Sad Ending

Day 1

At the end of Chapter 30, David has reconciled friendships in Israel.

Read   I Samuel 31.

CHECK OUT THE MAP!

Explanations in your reading:

v. 10   ". . . temple of Ashtoreths. . ." These are false goddesses.

v. 10   ". . . the wall of Beth Shan." This is Northern Israel territory. See your map.

v. 11   ". . . the inhabitants of Jabesh Gilead. . ." Saul protected these men from the Ammonites. These men are grateful to Saul. See 1 Samuel 11.

Write a summary and your own thoughts of the reading:

_____

_____

_____

_____

And so is the end of King Saul. The way King Saul dies was similar to the way he lived. Saul always took matters into his own hands. He never had total faith in God. Saul relied on his own plans.   He dwelt on his anger and jealousy instead of on the power and love of God. Saul constantly forgot God because he constantly thought of himself.

At Saul's last breath, he chooses, once again, to be in control.
The Bible tells nothing of any final words to God, no prayer at all.

Saul was rarely *trying* to be bad. He never *intended* to be an evil king. However, he gave God very little time. At times when Saul did inquire of the Lord, Saul did not have time to wait for an answer. He took matters into his own sinful hands and made many damaging decisions.

• • • • • •

Day 2

Apply & Obey

Here is a question for some deep thought: do you think you ever live your life sort of, kind of, maybe somewhat, a bit like, a little like Saul? Thoughtfully (not quickly) answer the following questions:

Do you ever fear that someone may be better than you? _____

Have you ever thought you deserved more or better than others? _____

Have you ever been jealous of someone else?

_____

Have you made decisions without talking it over with

God? _____

Have you wished for praise and glory from others?

_____

Have you done good works in hopes to be looked at,

seen, praised, or glorified by others? _____

Have you left God out of a whole day? _____

Have you disobeyed God? _____

Have you spoken disrespectfully of or to a church leader? _____

Have you taken advice from someone who is not a Christian, be it someone

you know or someone on TV? _____

Read

Apply

Obey

Pray

More than likely, at least half of these were answered with a heavy-hearted "yes." Like Saul, we often put ourselves first. These sins are of our flesh. We want to make ourselves happy. Saul represents our flesh. Our own beings, our flesh, or the Saul-"ish" part of us usually dares not to hurt others, just as long as we get what we want.

Only through Jesus Christ, we receive the Holy Spirit that will guide us when these selfish, "Saulish" sins arise in our hearts. Remember, the Holy Spirit will guide you.

LIVE IT!

Take a moment to think of God's grace that saves you, then pray and ask for the Holy Spirit. Then, read the questions above again.
Which ones do you need to ask God for forgiveness?

_____

_____

_____

Which sins may be hard for you to stop doing?

_____

_____

_____

Ask for the Holy Spirit to help you now.

Are there any questions above that you seem to keep thinking about?

_____

_____

_____

If so, that is the Holy Spirit working in you. There is something He wants you to see and know. Why do you think the Holy Spirit wants you to keep thinking about this?

_____

_____

_____

• • • • • •

Day 3

165

Write **Psalm 40:8** below and memorize.

_____

_____

_____

_____

Also, write the words of Jesus' prayer in **Luke 22:42**, and memorize.

_____

_____

_____

_____

Once memorized, share the verses with three people and add to your index cards and/or memory verses list.

_____

Pray however the Holy Spirit is guiding you.

_____

The Way I See It...

by Christopher Foster

There was one major difference between Saul seeking God and getting no answer, and David seeking God and getting an answer, and that difference was motive. Saul was seeking God not as a selfless, God-fearing being; but instead, Saul would seek God only when he felt he could not solve his problems by himself. David was just the opposite. Regardless of the severity of David's problems, he chose to seek God first, and God listened.

*The same holds true for me as a Christian man. I am to seek God in **all** that I do. It is very easy for me as a man to want to hedge and control my own destiny, without any intervention from the Lord. However, this is not possible. Paul says in 2 Corinthians 3:5, "Not that we are sufficient of ourselves to think of anything as being from ourselves, but our sufficiency is from God." We will never as Christian men live to the magnitude in which God has planned for us until we put Him first in **all** that we do!*

Lesson 2
Makin' Music

Day 1

The death of Saul closes the Book of I Samuel. His reign and kingdom have come to an end. Guess what happens.....

Read II Samuel 1.

Explanations in your reading:

v.2 ". . . fell to the ground and prostrated himself. . ." The exhausted man bowed to David. You may have the words "did obeisance" in your Bible version. This means to honor.

v. 10 ". . . So I killed him." No, he did not. This man is lying.

v.11 ". . . took hold of his own clothes and tore them. . ." It was once a tradition to tear one's clothes as a sign of mourning, and to express how someone's heart may be "torn" because of the death of a loved one. Tearing clothes was a common practice all throughout the Bible. Just in case you're thinking about it, the answer is no. Do not pull a "But Mom, I'm in mourning."

Write a summary and your own thoughts of the reading:

_____

_____

_____

_____

_____

• • • • • •

Day 2

The song was written as a memorial for the fallen King Saul and his son Jonathan. David was a great lover of music. "Psalm" means "song." David wrote at least 73 of the songs in the Book of Psalms, and he possibly wrote many of the Psalms that do not have an author's name under the chapter. He loved to write music! Not only that, he loved to play music! He was a talented harpist.

Do you have favorite praise songs? What are they? Try to list at least two songs (*praise* songs):

1. _____

2. _____

What is it about the songs you listed that you like?

_____

_____

_____

Apply & Obey

LIVE IT!

Use your voice or another instrument you are skilled at and learn all the words and/or notes to one of your favorite praise songs. Now, this may be out of your comfort zone, particularly if you are not one to sing, dance, and play 10 different instruments. Nonetheless, it is good to memorize praise songs. **Do not skip this important activity**. You do not have to have a voice like an angel to sing, and you do not have to be a professional musician to make music to the Lord. He hears the music in your heart the loudest.

Just think of how great God is: how He has protected you, how He loves you, how He gave His Son for you, how He created everything. Music is a gift to you **from God.** It is one of the most beautiful expressions of your heart and of God's love. Take this beautiful gift He has given you and praise Him!
What praise song do you choose to sing or play?

_____

Find the music on the internet, or you may write the lyrics here:

_____
_____
_____
_____
_____
_____
_____
_____
_____
_____
_____
_____
_____
_____
_____
_____
_____

•　•　•　•　•　•

Day 3

There are so many amazing verses about music. In many of the verses, God actually commands us to make music.

LIVE IT!

Read each of the following verses and select a favorite (or favorites) to memorize and to underline in your Bible:

Exodus 15:1   I will sing to the LORD, For He has triumphed gloriously!

Psalm 68:4   Sing to God, sing praises to His name.

Psalm 95:1	Oh come, let us sing to the LORD! Let us shout joyfully to the Rock of our salvation.
Psalm 101:1	I will sing of mercy and justice; to You, O LORD, I will sing praises.
Psalm 105:2	Sing to Him, sing psalms to Him; talk of His wondrous works!
Psalm 105:3	Glory in His holy name; Let the hearts of those rejoice who seek the LORD!
Psalm 71:23	My lips shall greatly rejoice when I sing to You, and my soul, which You have redeemed.
Psalm 150	1 Praise the LORD! Praise God in His sanctuary; Praise Him in His mighty firmament! 2 Praise Him for His mighty acts; Praise Him according to His excellent greatness! 3 Praise Him with the sound of the trumpet; Praise Him with the lute and harp! 4 Praise Him with the timbrel and dance; Praise Him with stringed instruments and flutes! 5 Praise Him with loud cymbals; Praise Him with clashing cymbals! 6 Let everything that has breath praise the LORD! Praise the LORD!

Ephesians 5:19   [Speak] to one another in psalms and hymns and spiritual songs, singing and making melody in your heart to the Lord.

Write your favorite verse from above here, and memorize:

_____

_____

_____

_____

Share the verse with three people, and add to your index cards and/or memory verses list.

God loves music. Getting closer to God's heart includes music that praises Him.

· · · · · ·
Day 4

Read and enjoy **Psalm 18**, which was God-inspired and written by David. Underline any passages you like, or any passages that help you feel closer to God. If you would like, write your thoughts and a summary of the chapter.

_____

_____

_____

_____

_____

_____

Pray and thank God for the gift of music.
Take time to pray about anything and everything in your heart.

The Way I See It...

by Christopher Foster

David paid tribute to Saul after his death for two reasons. First, David understood that Saul was anointed by God as king of Israel. Second, David was humble in nature. In Philippians 2:3, Paul says, "Let nothing be done through selfish ambition or conceit, but in lowliness of mind let each esteem others better than himself." "Lowliness of mind" in this verse means to be humble. This is one of my favorite verses in the Bible. As Christian men, we are to have a sense of humility. Through Jesus, David understood the importance of being humble, and so should we.

Lesson 3

You Talkin' To Me?

Day 1

Read II Samuel 2.

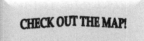

Explanations of your reading:

Here is a quick history lesson in reference to Judah and Gilead: The Book of Genesis tells us that before Israel (Jacob) died, he blessed his 12 sons, including some grandsons. Each son/grandson was blessed with and received, in time, their own families, and they formed their own tribes. These tribes later became slaves in Egypt until Moses led them (again, in time) to the land of Israel. After Moses died, Joshua and the tribes conquered the land of Israel and each tribe was allotted some territory.

Judah was one of those tribes, which was allotted land which contains cities, such as Bethlehem, Jerusalem, and Hebron.

Gilead is not the name of a son, or a grandson of Israel. Gilead was mostly in the tribe of Gad. This area was not very populated because it was a rocky mountain region. Nevertheless, Gilead was the name given to this region.

Think of Israel as a country, such as the United States of America. Think of Judea and Gilead as the states. Think of places such as Jabesh-Gilead, Bethlehem, and Hebron as cities in different states.

So, there is your history/geography lesson. Biblical history is interesting. Understanding exactly where all these things are taking place helps your reading make much more sense.

> v. 8-9   These places are on your map. Ephraim and Benjamin were
>   territories in Israel.
> v.12   Gibeon was in the Benjamite tribe/territory, not a city, which is
>   just north of Judea.

In your reading, there are many people introduced in chapter 2. It is time to meet them:

2 Kingdoms

David	**Ishbosheth** (Saul's son)
in Judah	**in Jabesh-Gilead & all of Israel (except Judah)**
Joab – commander of army	Abner – commander of army
Abishai – brother of Joab	
Asahei – brother of Joab	

Write a summary and your own thoughts of the reading:

_____

_____

_____

_____

• • • • • •

Day 2

What you learn in this chapter are many details of a battle – how they fight and how many die. Many more men of King Ishbosheth die compared to the fallen men of King David **(yes, *King* David!)**.

Apply & Obey

The battle started with an arrogant, self-seeking bully named Abner. Joab was the one being bullied.

Here are some present-day ways Abner would challenge Joab:

1. "You think you're tough? Prove it!"

2. "What are you, a Jesus freak?"

3. "Why are you so scared? Try it!"

4. "You're a wimp if you say no!"

5. "Your parents will never know!"

Read

Apply

Obey

Pray

Here is a promise: this world will say these things. It will happen. They will try to make you feel small and unmanly. No young man wants to be told he is not a man. It may seem that you have to give in to a challenge just to prove to someone you are tough and strong. Even our Savior Jesus Christ was tempted. Boy, did He ever prove His toughness!

LIVE IT!

Here are some answers to rest on in times of temptations:

1. "The joy of the Lord is my strength. God wants to give you that strength, too."

2. "I know God has a great plan for my life, so I choose to follow His way. Have you ever made that choice?"

3. "I *am* scared of what will happen if I do not walk with God; but I have no fear as I walk with Him."

4. "The Bible says I have to make a choice, too! I would feel like a wimp choosing the wrong way. I choose Jesus!"

5. "The Bible tells me to honor my parents when they are around *and* not around. My heavenly Father knows, and He is who we all ultimately answer to."

Do not shout these answers with a finger shaking in a bully's face. Do not say these words followed with a kick or spit and then run away for dear life. When someone is belittling you, stand strong and calm. Remember that this person may not know the Lord, and does not know how to be obedient to God. This person may have no joy of knowing Jesus. Your answer will make you stronger in Christ and may turn some "bullies" toward Jesus.

Read **1 Peter 3:13-18**. Write 1 Peter 3:15 below and memorize.

_____

_____

_____

_____

_____

After memorizing, share the verse with three people and add to your index cards and/or memory verses list.

_____

Pray for someone you know
that may not have a relationship with God through Jesus Christ.

_____

Chapter 9

Blessings

I am so grateful that the Lord has placed this book in your path. I want God to use you. Being a vessel for God is such a blessing. Being a servant for God is never a chore or an obligation; it is a blessing, a gift from God Almighty!

I pray that you are blessed with great insight into God's heart. I pray that you feel courageous and secure as you are growing into a man of God.

Remember your blessings by sharing them. Tell others the great things you know about God. Share the Bible by telling others some of the great Bible verses you have learned from this study.

This chapter and book will end with David becoming King of Israel – all of Israel. However, I encourage you not to put your Bible down once this book is over. Continue to read about the life of David, or go back and read the first part of I Samuel. It is so interesting.

Ask a friend or parent to read the rest of David's life and/or I Samuel with you, and learn God's truth together.

Israel

II Samuel 3, 4, & 5

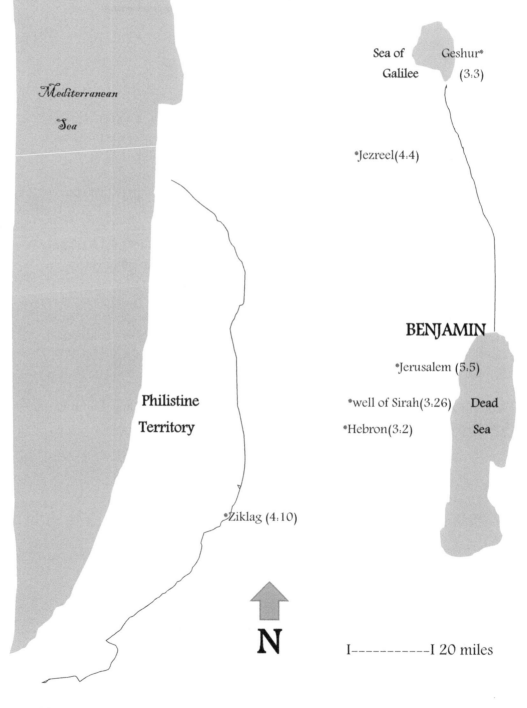

Mediterranean

Sea

Sea of
Galilee

Geshur*
(3:3)

*Jezreel(4:4)

BENJAMIN

*Jerusalem (5:5)

*well of Sirah(3:26)

Dead

Sea

*Hebron(3:2)

Philistine

Territory

*Ziklag (4:10)

N

I-----------I 20 miles

Lesson 1

First and Foremost!

Day 1

Read II Samuel 3:1-5.

Write a summary and your own thoughts of the reading:

_____

_____

_____

_____

_____

. . . . . .

Day 2

David's multiple marriages at once are today called polygamy, which in most parts of the world today is illegal. It was not illegal during David's reign, but it was still a sin. Commandment 7 of the Ten Commandments given to Moses in Exodus 20 commands, "Do not commit adultery." Yet David did.

We do the same today. That is, we disobey commandments, particularly those that are not against the law. For example,. . .

Commandment 1: Worship the one true God. This commandment is greatly disobeyed in our country, yet no one says anything. As a matter of fact, Christians are condemned for their belief of and obedience to this commandment.

Now here's another big one:

Commandment 2: Do not make idols for yourself. Many people break this commandment and yet do not see it broken.

An idol is anything you do or have in your life that #1, is not for God, but completely for you; #2, is more a part of your life than God is; and #3, is something that deep in your heart you consider more important than God.

For example, if you spend more time with video games every day than you do in time with God or for God, the video games are an idol. There is nothing wrong with playing video games and being determined to reach high scores. Have fun! Enjoy life! Video games are not necessarily separate from God. If you play with a grateful heart and share with friends or siblings, or if you play with the understanding that you will not let the video games consume a big chunk of your days, then enjoy your fun time. However, when you choose to take from God the time HE alone has given you and spend it separated from Him, you reflect your relationship with God.

How important is it? Have you ever thought of what it would be like to have no relationship with God and no way of having one? No God, no hope, no protection, no forgiveness, no miracles, no love, no eternity. Just fear, hate, loss, anguish, death, oh, and did I mention fear?

Apply & Obey

What would *honestly* hurt you most? (Circle your answer.)

Losing TV	or	Losing God;
Losing video games	or	Losing God
Losing your favorite books	or	Losing God
Losing a hobby/interest	or	Losing God
Losing your pool, trampoline, camper..	or	Losing God
Losing your home	or	Losing God
Losing your best friend	or	Losing God
Losing your pet	or	Losing God

Losing a family member   or   Losing God

Losing part of your own body   or   Losing God

These are tough choices, but this will show you how close your relationship is with God.
How close is it?

_____

_____

_____

Do you want to make your relationship with God stronger?

_____

Magnify the Lord!

Look up the word "magnify." Write the definition:

_____

_____

_____

Do not beat yourself up if it's hard for you to put God before something else you love or someone else you love. These things and people you love are blessings from God. These blessings have helped you become the wonderful young man you are today. However, they are all temporary. As sad as it seems, the things on earth will be gone. Yet God is eternal. Now that you are growing into a man, your love for God needs to be first in your life.

The remaining 8 commandments are easy to understand, but are often hard to obey. To disobey just seems more "normal" in our world and in our own lives.

•   •   •   •   •   •

Day 3

Read **Psalm 119:1-24.** Choose *one* verse to memorize and write it here:

_____

_____

_____

_____

_____

After you have memorized the verse, share it with three people, and add the verse to your memory verses list and/or index cards.

Pray for God to show you when you disobey.
Thank God for His commandments that
keep you close to Him.

Lesson 2
A Smidge of Humility

Day 1

Read II Samuel 3:6-39.

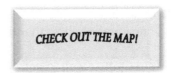
CHECK OUT THE MAP!

Explanations in your reading:

v.7   "... concubine. . ." Many great Godly men had concubines in the Bible, including the late Saul. A concubine was a woman who was like a servant to the man or woman of the house, and was also an intimate "girlfriend" to the man of the house. Remember, they lived at a time when polygamy was considered normal life.

v.7-10   Ishbosheth accused Abner of committing adultery with Saul's old concubine Rizpah. Abner fumes with anger for being accused, and swears to join forces with King David and help destroy King Ishbosheth's kingdom.

Write a summary and your own thoughts of the reading:

_____

_____

_____

_____

_____

• • • • • •

Day 2

Think about David and Abner – they were not necessarily friends, nor did they associate with each other for a long time. They did not grow up together. They were not family. Yet, King David immensely mourned for Abner after his murder.

David respected this man Abner. David acknowledged his hard work to strengthen King Saul's kingdom. David was grateful to Abner for his help in David's kingdom.

Don't you think it is interesting that David is sorrowful..., no, *beyond* sorrow and sadness, because Abner died? "I am weak today," David replied. Much like the late King Saul, Abner was highly revered by King David, showing his concern not only for himself, but also for others.

The people of Judah noticed this love and concern in their King, and they liked it! Their king cared for others. That's a good trait for a King. It is an important trait for any young man seeking after the heart of God.

Read this carefully: loving and caring for others above yourself shows humility. Not humiliation. Humility. Humility is believing that all of who you are comes from *God alone.*

Apply & Obey

In each of the following verses, a box is given for you to add the names of your brothers, sisters, mom, dad, neighbor, friend at school, enemy at school, whomever's name you feel the Lord may be leading you to write. After adding these names in each box, *read the verse aloud* using the names you wrote as part of the Bible verse.

Matthew 22:39   "You shall love [   ] as yourself."

Matthew 25:40   ". . . inasmuch as you did it to [   ],
My brethren, you did it to Me."

1 Corinthians 10:24   Let no one seek his own, but each one [   ]
's well-being.

Philippians 2:3,4   Let nothing be done through selfish ambition or conceit,

but in lowliness of mind let each esteem [   ] better than himself.

LIVE IT!

Repeat each verse aloud with the name of someone you know.

Choose one of the four verses to memorize, and share the verse with three people. Include the verse to your memory verses list and/or include the verse in your index cards.

Read

Apply

Obey

Pray

---

*Pray asking God to help you esteem others
and to love and care for others.
Pray for God's blessings on the names you wrote in the boxes.*

Lesson 3
Authority is a Really Good Word!

Day 1

Read II Samuel 4.

Explanations in your reading:

> v.2, 3   Baanah and Rechab – this is two brothers from the Benjamin tribe
> – two "bad news" brothers.

Write a summary and your own thoughts of the reading:

_____

_____

_____

_____

_____

. . . . . .

Day 2

Loads of stabbings and murders going on in these chapters, wouldn't you agree?
Answer the following questions:

What territory did King Ishbosheth rule over?

_____

What territory did King David rule over?

_____

Which King had a relationship with God?

_____

Which King was following God's will?

_____

Did David ever order for Ishbosheth's kingdom to be destroyed?

_____

Did David respect the kingdom of Ishbosheth?

_____

Respecting authority is a Godly act, practiced even by our Savior Jesus Christ. The authority in all of our lives includes our government, our teachers, our law-enforcement, our preachers, our parents, our caregivers, and our grandparents.

We will not always agree with or like the commands and guidance that each of these authority figures gives us. It may make no sense, and it may not seem fair. Nonetheless, as long as the commands are not against the Holy Scriptures, we need to obey. It is good practice. Practice is necessary for when *the real deal comes*...

For example, you practice a sport to be prepared for a game. You practice music to be prepared for a performance. In the same way, you practice obedience and respect to the authority in your life to be prepared for the commands and guidance of the Ultimate Authority.

God has a plan for you and for the world, and you must respect and obey authority now. Later will be too difficult to respect and obey God, particularly when God's commands make no sense to you, *or* when they do not seem fair, *or* when God wants you to wait for an answer, *or* when He answers you opposite of what you asked, *or* when His plans for your life do not completely match your own plans. If you do not practice honor and respect for authority right now, my precious brother, here's a forewarning, you will be miserable.

Do you remember at the beginning of the Bible study you learned that David was a man after God's own heart, and in order to know what is in God's heart, you need to know how to see things through His eyes? Think for moment about how God sees the world, your neighbors, the kids at your school, the family you know that has so many needs. How does God see them? Now, answer this question: Why is it so important to God that you obey?

_____

_____

_____

_____

Does your answer include the teachings in **Mark 16:15**? (An important verse to take the time to look up.)

• • • • • •

Day 3

Apply & Obey

The fifth commandment cannot be shouted loud enough, and it comes with a promise to you from God: "Honor your father and your mother that your days may be long upon the land which the LORD your God is giving you."

You may think, "Why should I respect and honor people who are sinners, like the president, or my teacher, or my parents?" It is a very good question with an important answer. First of all, the truth is our authority figures often make poor choices. Remember Romans 3:23. . . "All have sinned. . ." This includes authority. However, these people are in authority positions ONLY because God allows their placement or has placed them as your authorities Himself. God is the Ultimate Authority.

Now let us practice for when the real deal comes! This is a lesson in manners. Here are **three** great ways to practice respecting authority:

1. **Use words of respect.** "Yes sir/ma'am; No sir/ma'am. No more "yeahs," "na-ahs," "ahas," "nopes," "umm-hmms," "whatevers," "I haven't a clue," and no snorts or head nods and shakes. Yes, it is time for that authoritative finger. . .

LIVE IT!

Here's your challenge: Every time you fail to answer your parents with respect, repeat "Yes/no ma'am/sir" 50 times. For example, if you answer, "Yeah," to your Dad, then you must repeat "Yes sir," 50 times aloud. It is silly and inconvenient, which is why it works! It will help you to start to remember to answer with respect. Ask your parents to hold you accountable.

This is to help your heart grow, not for fashion. In other words, if you practice words of respect continuously every day, it will become more a part of you and more of a habit (habitually). Then, it will grow important in your heart.

2. **Always look authority** (or actually anyone) **in the eye** when one of you is speaking. Stop whatever you are doing to listen. Do not look around. Acknowledge the time the person is taking to spend with you and look at them. Give them your full, undivided attention.

3. **Always answer in complete sentences** to parents, other authority figures, and adults. This may sound silly, but here is an example:
   Parent: "How was school today?"
   You: "OK."

   What? What was that? At the very least, here is a more respectful way to answer:
   Parent: "How was school today?"
   You: "School was OK today, Mom."
   Although a terribly plain answer, do you see how the complete sentence sounds more respectful?

LIVE IT!

Now you try. Have a parent read these questions to you. Your job is to answer aloud in *complete* sentences.

1. How are you today?
2. How did you sleep last night?
3. Do you plan on going to church?
4. Did you like 1 Samuel or 2 Samuel better?
5. Do you want hot dogs for dinner?
6. Will you clean the bathroom please?
7. Do you know what happened to my plant?
8. What is your favorite color?
9. Did you brush your teeth?
10. Did you finish all your homework?

If you answer these questions like a robot, it may be because you do not normally answer in complete sentences, so it may seem strange.

Answering in complete sentences is not a command in the Bible. Neither is saying "sir" and "ma'am," and neither is making eye contact. However, it is a way of practicing respect to authority. When you take the time to answer in complete sentences, you are showing that you respect the request and need for an answer, and you take time to give them what they are asking for.

· · · · · ·

Day 4

The three ways of practicing respect listed above will in turn help equip you to honor, respect, revere, and obey God.

LIVE IT!

Write out and memorize **2 Timothy 2:15**:

_____

_____

_____

_____

_____

After you have memorized the verse, share it with three people and add to your list of memory verses and/or index cards.

_____

Pray for all the authority in your life,

and ask God to help you respect and obey authority.

_____

Lesson 4
Take note!

Day 1

Read II Samuel 5:1-5.

Triumph!   Now that you know all that David went through, the suffering, the anger, the loneliness, the perseverance, don't these verses give you a good feeling?

Write a summary and your own thoughts of the reading:

_____

_____

_____

_____

• • • • • •

Day 2

David was just a boy, a shepherd boy, when Samuel anointed him King of Israel. David had to suffer and see and learn a whole lot before all of Israel revered and hailed him as their King.

As David kept his relationship close to God, he wrote about it.

• When David *felt alone*, he wrote about it:

Psalm 13:1 "How long, O LORD? Will You forget me forever? How long will You hide Your face from me?"

- When David *felt safe* in God's arms, he wrote about it:
  Psalm 71:5 "For You are my hope, O LORD God; You are my trust from my youth."

- When David *felt God's strength*, he wrote about it:
  Psalm 18:32 "It is God who arms me with strength, and makes my way perfect."

- When David *felt confused and unsafe*, he wrote about it:
  Psalm 3:7 "Arise, O LORD; Save me, O my God!"

- When David *just wanted to love God*, he wrote about it:
  Psalm 9:1 "I will praise you, O LORD, with my whole heart."

There were so many situations in David's life, and God inspired David to write it all down. God knew that the words in the Book of Psalms would draw David closer to Him.

Also, as God inspired these words for David to write, God was thinking of you. God knew your eyes would one day see those words. Just as David searched for the very heart of God, you were there. You were in God's heart. Now that you are growing into a man, just as King David did, seek God. Seek Him!

Read

Apply

Obey

Pray

Apply & Obey

There is one more challenge for you that will hopefully continue throughout your life. . .

LIVE IT!

Keep a journal. A journal is any type of notebook that you use to write down your thoughts pertaining to your growth in God. If you are stumped on what to write, here are some ideas:

1. Write about why you are sad, scared, lonely, frustrated, or angry.

195

2. Write a thank you letter to God.
3. Write down what you think of God.
4. Write down a verse you have read in the Bible that you would like to remember.
5. Write a prayer request to God.
6. Make a list of blessings from God.
7. Write out memory verses.
8. Write down something someone said to you that you would like to remember.
9. Write down how you would like God to help you grow.
10. Write down a list of reasons why you love God.
11. Write down an answer you feel God is giving you.
12. Write a prayer about someone you have been thinking about.
13. Write down a Bible verse that confuses you, and why.
14. Thank God for your parents, particularly your dad, in writing.
15. Write about an event where you knew God was there.
16. Write down some things you heard in a sermon that you want to remember.
17. Write down what you hope your future will be like.
18. Write down your wishes and dreams.
19. Write down ways you are growing closer to God.
20. Write a list of things and people to pray for.
21. Write about your favorite missionary.
22. Write about another Christian you look up to, and that you would like to be like.
23. Write about your future wife.
24. Write out the words to a praise song you really like.
25. Write a list of things you would like to do for God.

David wrote down a lot of these same things, and God worked amazingly in David's life.

Always remember to write the date in your journal entry. Your writing does not have to be long. It does not have to be fancy. It will not be graded. It is between you and God. Just be honest. Write what is in your heart.

Try to be consistent in your writing. Keep your journal handy and always in the same place, such as in your bedroom. Choose a time to write (morning, after school, bedtime . . .). Make a goal for yourself of how often you will write. Maybe two times per week, maybe every day. Read your Bible before or after your journal writing.

Keeping a journal allows you to express your heart. Then, once you have your thoughts written, you can read it and see what is in your heart. Oftentimes, through your writing, you will find an answer or guidance from God. Sometimes, you may feel inspired by God to write down something in particular just as David did.

However, if you abhor writing, or if you believe scrubbing toilets, scrubbing floors, and matching socks can bring you more bliss than journal-writing, there may still be a solution.

Now, hold fast… you will still need a pen. You will also need your Bible. By the way, daily Bible reading is a must, whether you like to read or not. As you read, underline verses you like. Make a small note in your Bible beside the verse. With keywords, insert things from the list above in your Bible.

After months of journal writing, go back and read how your relationship with God has grown. You will see how God's hands have worked in your life, as you, my precious eternal brother in Christ, become a man after God's own heart!

Our very last memory verse is words from our Lord and Savior Jesus Christ:

Write **Matthew 6:33** and memorize:

_____

_____

_____

_____

_____

Once memorized, share the verse with three people and add the verse to your memory verses list and/or index cards.

Write your own prayer here:

_____

_____

_____

_____

_____

_____

I pray that you never stop seeking more of God, and that if you have not already, you let God forgive you of any and all sin through your faith by receiving Jesus as your Savior and your Lord. I pray that as you keep growing closer to God's heart, you can see things more clearly through God's eyes.

Appendix
List of Memory Verses
(NKJV)

Writing out memory verses is not just "busy work." As you write the verses out, it gives you a chance to focus on nothing else but the Word of God, and memorizing it.

Use this list as a checklist to make sure you have written every verse down on an index card or in your memory verses lists. I found many great FREE apps, and I plugged in these verses. Commit yourself to keep these verses alive in your life by making yourself read them and re-memorize them when you have down-time.

There are so many great ways to spend your free time. But do not forget about your memory verses. It is going to take a strong commitment from you to take the time to keep these verses in your heart.

Psalm 113:3   From the rising of the sun to its going down the LORD's name *is* to be praised.

Joshua 1:9   Have I not commanded you? Be strong and of good courage; do not be afraid, nor be dismayed, for the LORD your God *is* with you wherever you go.

Psalm 91:11, 12 For He shall give His angels charge over you, To keep you in all your ways.

James 4:8   Draw near to God and He will draw near to you.

I Timothy 4:12 Let no one despise your youth, but be an example to the believers in word, in conduct, in love, in spirit, in faith, in purity.

I Samuel 16:7b For the LORD does not not see as man sees; for man looks at the outward appearance, but the LORD looks at the heart.

Exodus 20:12   Honor your father and mother, that your days may be long upon the land which the LORD your God is giving you.

Psalm 133:1	Behold, how good and how pleasant it is For brethren to dwell together in unity!
Psalm 27:1	The LORD is my light and my salvation; Whom shall I fear? The LORD is the strength of my life; Of whom shall I be afraid?
Psalm 115:1	Not unto us, O LORD, not unto us, But to Your name give glory, Because of Your Mercy, Because of Your truth.
Psalm 84:10a	For a day in Your courts is better than a thousand.

Ephesians 6:13-20

[13] Therefore take up the whole armor of God, that you may be able to withstand in the evil day, and having done all, to stand. [14] Stand therefore, having girded your waist with truth, having put on the breastplate of righteousness, [15] and having shod your feet with the preparation of the gospel of peace; [16] above all, taking the shield of faith with which you will be able to quench all the fiery darts of the wicked one. [17] And take the helmet of salvation, and the sword of the Spirit, which is the word of God; [18] praying always with all prayer and supplication in the Spirit, being watchful to this end with all perseverance and supplication for all the saints— [19] and for me, that utterance may be given to me, that I may open my mouth boldly to make known the mystery of the gospel, [20] for which I am an ambassador in chains; that in it I may speak boldly, as I ought to speak.

Psalm 84:10a	For a day in Your courts is better than a thousand.
I John 4:7, 8	Beloved, let us love one another, for love is of God; and everyone who loves is born of God and knows God. He who does not love does not know God, for God is love.

Matthew 5:43-48

[43] "You have heard that it was said, 'You shall love your neighbor and hate your enemy.' [44] But I say to you, love your enemies, bless those who curse you, do good to those who hate you, and pray for those who spitefully use you and persecute you [45] that you may be sons of your Father in heaven; for He makes His sun rise on the evil and on the good, and sends rain on the just and on the unjust. [46] For if

you love those who love you, what reward have you? Do not even the tax collectors do the same? [47] And if you greet your brethren[s] only, what do you do more *than others?* Do not even the tax collectors do so? [48] Therefore you shall be perfect, just as your Father in heaven is perfect.

Ephesians 2:8 For by grace you have been saved through faith, and that not of yourselves; it is the gift of God.

Psalm 120:2 Deliver my soul, O LORD, from lying lips
And from a deceitful tongue.

Romans 8:1 There is therefore now no condemnation to those who are in Christ Jesus, who do not walk according to the flesh, but according to the Spirit.

Psalm 22:22 I will declare Your name to my brethren;
In the midst of the assembly I will praise You.

Jeremiah 33:3 Call to Me, and I will answer you, and show you great and mighty things, which you do not know.

Romans 11:36 For of Him and through Him and to Him are all things, to whom be glory forever. Amen.

Colossians 3:23 And whatever you do, do it heartily, as to the Lord and not to men.

Matthew 25:40 And the King will answer and say to them, 'Assuredly, I say to you, inasmuch as you did it to one of the least of these My brethren, you did it to Me.'

Psalm 55:22 Cast your burden on the LORD,
And He shall sustain you;
He shall never permit the
Righteous to be moved.

I Samuel 26:24 "And indeed, as your life was valued much this day in my eyes, so let my life be valued much in the eyes of the LORD, and let Him deliver me out of all tribulation."

Deuteronomy 20:4 For the LORD your God is He who goes with you, to fight for you against your enemies, to save you.

Galatians 6:9   And let us not grow weary while doing good, for in due season we shall reap if we do not lose heart.

Proverbs 11:27 He who earnestly seeks good finds favor,
But trouble will come to him who seeks evil.

Psalm 40:8   I delight to do Your will, O my God,
And Your law is within my heart.

Luke 22:42   Father, if it is Your will, take this cup away from Me; nevertheless not My will, but Yours be done.

II Timothy 2:15 Be diligent to present yourself approved to God, a worker who does not need to be ashamed, rightly dividing the word or truth.

Matthew 6:33   But seek first the kingdom of God and His righteousness, and all these things shall be added to you.

Luke 10:2   Then He said to them, "The harvest truly is great, but the laborers are few; therefore pray the Lord of the harvest to send out laborers into His harvest."

You also chose a verse to memorize that dealt with praising God through songs, and you chose another verse in Psalm 119.

Extra Writing Room for you:

_____

_____

_____

_____

_____

_____

_____

_____

_____

_____

_____

_____

_____

_____

_____

_____

_____

_____

_____

_____

_____

_____

_____

_____

_____

_____

About the Authors

Katy Foster lives in Flowery Branch, Georgia, and is a homeschool mom of three children, Alex, Annabelle, and Ansley. All that she writes is out of her love for her own children, and she is compelled through her writing to share the love of God through Jesus Christ with others. She and her husband, Chris Foster, are members of Blackshear Place Baptist Church, where their heart of worship is primarily through serving and praising God with the children.

Christopher Foster, the husband of Katy Foster, is an elementary school administrator. He is salt and a light for Jesus for his hundreds of children that he helps to educate and provide care and love.

For more information, email Katy at digginwithKaty@gmail.com.

Made in the USA
Las Vegas, NV
14 March 2022

45615484R00122